Corn Snakes in Captivity
by Don Soderberg

Professional Breeder

E C O

ISBN 978-0-9767334-1-2

Copies available from:

ECO Herpetological Publishing & Distribution
4 Rattlesnake Canyon Rd., Rodeo, NM 88056 USA
telephone: 575.557.5757   fax: 575.557.7575
email: ecoorders@hotmail.com website: http://www.reptileshirts.com

Zoo Book Sales
http://www.zoobooksales.com

LIVING ART publishing   SOUTH MOUNTAIN REPTILES
http://www.livingartpublishing.com   http://www.cornsnake.NET

All photography by the author unless otherwise noted.

Design and layout by Russ Gurley.
Cover design by Rafael Porrata.

Printed in China.

Front Cover: A beautiful banded Okeetee Corn Snake. Photo by Don Soderberg.
Back Cover: An ultramel, the newest co-dominant Corn Snake morph. Photo by Don Soderberg.

DEDICATION

I am eternally grateful for my late parents' tolerance of all the wild animals my brother and I sneaked into our bedroom as kids. This book is dedicated to all parents that realize their children could be doing worse things than keeping snakes in the house.

ACKNOWLEGEMENTS

What you will see in the following pages is based upon my experiences as a keeper and breeder of corn snakes for over 30 years. As it is with most things we achieve in life, this book would not have been possible without the help of others.

First to be acknowledged for his contributions is my good friend, Steve Jones of El Paso, Texas. Without Steve's help and encouragement, this book would not have been written. Steve, I hope I'll always be there for you like you have been there for me.

Any wife that tolerates the time and dedication needed to maintain thousands of reptiles must be acknowledged. Tammie, not only could I never have done this without you, but I thank you for your help, your tolerance, and your unwavering faith in me.

Many friends, colleagues and fellow corn snake lovers unselfishly donated their time and talents when I needed them. I am honored to acknowledge the following people for their special contributions to *Corn Snakes in Captivity*.

My special thanks to Bob and Sheri Ashley for allowing *Corn Snakes in Captivity* to become a part of the growing ECO Professional Breeders Series.

Thank you, Russ Gurley for doing such a wonderful job of editing and design layout. It was an honor to work with you.

Bob Ashley, Sheri Ashley, David Barker, Tracy Barker, Daniel Bohle, Dianne Bolognani, Mark Britain, Darin Chappell, John Cherry, Edison Gabrintina, Michael Glaß, Russ Gurley, Connie Hurley, DVM, Joshua Ingram, Chris Killian, Samantha Lewis, Dr. Shawn Lockhard, Bill Love, Kathy Love, Mark Lucas, Terri Manning, Chad Martin, Marsha Campbell Mathews, Nathaniel Miller, Ryan Moss, Cord Offermann, DVM, Mark Perkins, Charles Pritzel, Justin Ratts, Sean Ratts, Don Shores, James Smith, Walter Smith, Jim Stelpflug, John Stolz, Ken Strasser, Adam Sweetman, Travis Whisler, Nancy Wimer, and Rich Zuchowski.

TABLE OF CONTENTS

INTRODUCTION

This very unusual Striped Hypomelanistic Lavender corn snake will be almost patternless as an adult.

GENERAL INFORMATION

No other snakes are kept as pets and bred in captivity more than corn snakes. There are several reasons for this distinguished reputation, but probably the most obvious and appreciated is that of their docile nature. Like all snakes, corns are not domesticated animals. Their natural benefit to humans is in the realm of rodent control. While corn snakes will never replace the dog as Man's best friend, they do have an impressive list of assets.

Tame . . . actually enjoy being handled
Harmless to humans . . . bites to humans are extremely rare and corn snakes are not venomous
Attractive . . . bright and colorful
Highly variable in color and pattern . . . over 100 combinations and counting
Small sized . . . average adults 3.5'- 4.5' long (107-138 cm)
Easy to feed . . . never need rodents larger than adult mice and generally only one weekly
Inexpensive to maintain . . . modest resources required compared to most household pets
Reasonably priced . . . $15.00 and up
Easily bred in captivity . . . minimal prerequisites to breeding

---

Note the similarity of this corn snake's belly pattern to an ear of Indian corn.

What's In a Name?

There are two common theories about how the corn snake got its name. One is that many years ago when harvested corn was stored at most homesteads, these rodentiferous serpents were frequently found in and around the corn cribs and grain storage bins where their favorite prey (mice and rats) were in abundance. The other says that it was named for the resemblance its belly has to an ear of Indian corn.

Corn snakes are classified in the family Colubridae, the largest serpent family and a mixed tribe of mostly harmless genera and species. On-going comparative studies of rat snakes have resulted in a proposed taxonoimic classification change that is gaining general acceptance (Collins, pers. com.).

Proposed is the removal of corn snakes from the genus *Elaphe* to the genus *Pantherophis* (Utiger et al., 2002). *Pantherophis* is an old name, originally proposed for North American rat snakes by Fitzinger in 1843. Since I agree that these races are sufficiently different enough to have separate genera, I will use the newly proposed Latin name of *Pantherophis guttatus* instead of the old name, *Elaphe guttata guttata*. An additional change is that the two taxa once recognized as subspecies of the corn snake (*emoryi* and *slowinskii*) are now recog-

A beautiful Okeetee Creamsicle from South Mountain Reptiles.

nized as full species (Burbrink, 2002), making corns the only member of the species *Pantherophis guttatus*. At this time, the Latin name change of most North American rat snakes is so recent that many websites and documents still label them with the former genus *Elaphe*, which now applies to rat snake species from Europe and Asia.

Where Are Corn Snakes Found?

The natural habitats preferred most by corn snakes are the pine forests and grasslands of the southeastern United States. Their basic geographic range is from the Florida Keys north to New Jersey and from the East Coast below New Jersey, westward to Arkansas and Louisiana. Corns are found in almost all floral facets within pine and deciduous forests. Their adaptation to Man's influence on the environment means they are also frequently found in many other settings where humans have changed the landscape. This includes back yards and corns are even found inside homes within their range. By virtue of their primary range in the southeastern United States, corns are obviously more adapted to humid environments than arid ones.

Note: Before airplane and ship transportation, corns were relegated to their natural habitats in the southeastern United States. Besides shipping and smuggling by humans, stowaways in cargo containers on planes, ships and

Corn snakes are arboreal in nature and can often be seen resting on the limbs of trees. Photo by Bill Love.

trucks have contributed to corn snakes showing up in many unexpected places around the world. In addition, escapees and even some that were purposely released into the wild are successfully living and in some cases procreating in foreign states and other countries around the world. This human-assisted transplantation is commonly referred to as "animal pollution".

Size and Age

Hatching out at a mere eight to 12" long (20-30 cm), corn snakes mature to an average length of approximately 48" (122 cm). If you stayed in this hobby for 20 years and saw more than 1,000 adults, you're not likely to see more than one or two specimens over 5.5' long (168 cm). Naturally, there are exceptions and the record is just over six feet (183 cm). A six foot long (1.8 m) corn is probably rarer than a human over eight feet tall.

In adult corns, males are generally larger than females. Females average 48" (122 cm) in length while males average 54" (138 cm).

Note: Measuring your snake's shed (*sloughed*) skin is not an accurate reflection of its actual length. Shed skins are sometimes as much as 40% larger than the snake.

Under average captive conditions and with proper feeding, a corn snake grows approximately 10-15" (25-38 cm) per year for the first two years. Growth usually slows for the next three years and most corns are almost fully grown at six years of age. Do not be alarmed if your snake does not follow conventional growth rates. It's not possible to accurately determine the age of any snake by measurement. Snakes are in a small fraternity of animals whose growth rate is commensurate to their food intake. Since they mature more in terms of size rather than age, terminology can sometimes vary within the industry. As a general rule, corns are called yearlings after turning one year old and sub-adults from that age up to approximately 36" (90 cm). These terms will be useful to the prospective buyer for getting an idea of the age or size of an advertised snake, based on popular corn snake jargon.

The average lifespan of a corn in captivity is 12 to 15 years, but the record is well over 20. With the advent of the Internet and the resulting increase of knowledge regarding nutrition and maintenance, I expect that longevity record to double in the years to come.

Chapter ONE: SELECTING YOUR CORN SNAKE

With proper education, even young children can safely handle corn snakes. Photo by Ryan Moss.

Like all pets, your corn snake will depend on you for its very health and welfare for many years. If you are not prepared to spend the appropriate money and time to keep it healthy, admire corns from afar. Just visit your friends' snakes or enjoy the collections at your local pet stores or zoos.

Note: Never give any pet to someone as a gift unless that person is fully aware of the maintenance requirements and is prepared to accept the responsibility. "Disposable Pet" mentality is a growing problem in the pet industry today. Some people acquire pets just for the fun of having them and when finances or time are not sufficient to properly care for that pet, they abuse or neglect it. This often results in the death of the animal.

The first thing you should do before acquiring any pet is thoroughly research all media resources available to you. Besides books and testimonies from friends and acquaintances, the Internet is a relative wealth of information. Just remember that not everything you read on the Internet is accurate. Research many sources and "blend" the information gathered before making decisions.

Below is a checklist you should use BEFORE acquiring your new corn snake.

* Thoroughly research care requirements
* Talk to corn snake owners for suggestions and care tips
* Acquire a secure cage and accessories
* Buy a supply of appropriately sized rodents
* Prepare drinking water (city tap water is not recommended)
* Test heating devices and thermometers
* Test cage closing/locking devices to reduce chances of escape

Care and caging requirements are detailed in the **HOUSING** and **FEEDING AND WATERING** chapters.

Captive-Bred vs. Wild-Caught

Most corn snakes in the pet trade today are produced in captivity, but since many states still allow harvesting of this species, it is not uncommon to see wild-caught specimens. In some states within their range, it's entirely legal to catch and possess corns. In other states, it's not only illegal to collect them from the wild, but it is breaking the law to possess one without a special permit. If you're considering capturing a corn snake from the wild, first check state and local regulations that may apply. Likewise, if you're considering purchasing and keeping any corn, check to be certain it's allowed where you live and if permits are required.

Captive-bred corn snakes are the smart choice for you and for the environment. Acquiring a corn that was hatched in captivity is more than just saving a wild one from being captured. The collecting of wild corns sometimes results in damage to their natural habitats. Some field collectors don't leave trees and landscapes in the same condition in which they found them. This can have a negative impact on all life forms within those ecosystems.

Generally speaking, corns produced in captivity are free of diseases and parasites. Most breeders of corns are very responsible about reducing or eliminating internal and external parasites. It's not only good for the health of the animals, but also good for the breeders' reputations.

Captive-hatched corn snakes are available in a wide range of colors and patterns.

Most wild-caught corns have parasites that could cause health problems. Of course, transference of disease and parasites to your other pets from cross handling is always a possibility. Therefore, if you do get a wild-caught corn, it's important to have it checked for parasites so you can eliminate them as quickly as possible.

Handling Corn Snakes

In an effort to lay out this book in the sequence of acquisition, it may seem out of place to discuss handling corn snakes here, but if you're acquiring your snake in person and are able to handle it first, here are some recommendations you may find helpful.

For reasons of sanitation, it is always recommended that you not only wash your hands and forearms after holding any animal, but you should also wash before handling snakes. This reduces the chances of transmitting germs from one snake to another and corns may become confused about alien smells that might be on your skin from handling objects or other animals. You should also refrain from eating food while handling snakes.

Snakes are no different from any other pets in terms of being able to transmit germs to humans. Like most animals, reptiles are potential carriers of bacteria and other pathogens (*causative agents of disease*) that can be harmful to us. Most susceptible to these are people with inferior immune systems. Children under five years of age or any person that is ill or suffers from immune-suppression should avoid handling any reptile. The most infamous bacterium associated with reptiles is *Salmonella*. These are more commonly associated with raw or undercooked foods such as meats and eggs, but can be contracted from infected reptiles as well. Do not allow any reptile to come in contact with your mouth and don't allow young children to handle corns unsupervised. Of course, you cannot contract anything from an uninfected source. To reduce the chance of such pathogens, keep the cage clean and practice sensible hygiene for you and your pets.

Biting

Like any animal, corn snakes are capable of biting. They have the best reputation among snakes for being tame, but they do have teeth and when provoked or stressed, they can bite. Most corns in the pet trade today have been selectively bred to be docile. On rare occasions, a corn snake hatches that just seems to want to bite everything that moves. When it's not possible to personally handle a corn prior to purchase, ask the seller if it has shown a propensity for biting.

After shipping or traveling home from a pet store or reptile show, corn snakes can be confused and stressed. Ensure that temperatures are correct and that you have been handling your new pet with clean hands. Sometimes it's a matter of the snake not yet being accustomed to the smell of your skin. If you suspect this to be the case, try putting an article of your clothing in the cage with the snake for several days. A shirt or glove you've been wearing should have enough of your scent on it to help your new corn become familiar with you.

Another common reason for corns biting humans is from enticement or confusion about smells. Sometimes feeding reactions cause them to non-maliciously "bite the hand that feeds them". After thoroughly washing with soap and water, rinse off all soap residues and dry your hands and forearms prior to handling your pet. Ordinarily the smell of human skin will not provoke aggression or biting, but corns will some-times react aggressively to seemingly benign odors on your skin. That sandwich you just ate, the tire you just changed, or even the cat you just petted. Avoid handling any other animals prior to picking up your corn as this can elicit aggression. A corn's most trusted sense is that of smell. If your hand smells like prey or predator, you could be bitten.

If you are bitten by a corn snake, don't panic. I've never heard of the bite from a corn snake requiring medical attention beyond routine cleansing and covering with an adhesive bandage. With six rows of tiny teeth, the chance of the bite from a corn snake penetrating your skin and causing bleeding is good. Most of the damage from such bites is the result of your instant reaction to pull away from the snake. When you pull back quickly, some of the teeth can cut and/or break off in your skin. Being essentially colorless, tooth parts that embed in your skin are sometimes initially difficult to find and remove. The bite site around a tooth in your skin will fester after a few days, making the tooth fragment easier to locate and extract. In the rare occasion in which the snake will not release its bite grip, you have a few options. Hold very still and it should realize you are far too large to consume and consequently relax its mouth. If that doesn't work, go directly to the sink and run cold water on the head of the snake. This usually causes them to open their mouth quickly. If not, you can slowly add warmer water to the situation. Rarely should you need to resort to hot water and obviously this would not be safe for your snake. The teeth are curved inward so as to embed deeper when their prey attempts to free itself from the snake's grip. Hence, pulling away from the snake can break off teeth and cause more damage to you and to your corn.

It is not wise to handle a corn snake that is about to shed. The shedding process takes approximately 10 days from when you first notice an overall opaque or milky look to when it sheds the old skin. More on this subject is detailed in the **SHEDDING** chapter.

When reaching to pick up a corn, approach it without delay. Sometimes, if you're slow to pick up a corn or make hesitating gestures in the process, it might distrust your intentions. Not being social animals, all snakes are naturally suspicious when in close proximity to any animal larger than themselves. Pick up your corn mid-body without hesitation. Do not attempt to grab it by the neck or tail as these are the most sensitive parts of a snake. Snakes instinctively know these are the two most likely targets of attack by predators. The best way to pick up the snake is to put your fingers under it and lift it out of the cage. Letting its body rest on your hand instead of constraining it by

grasp reduces the chance of the snake misidentifying you as a predator. If you're not pinching or otherwise hurting it, the *ride* on your
hand is perceived as being non-hostile. In the process of lifting them
from the cage, they have time to recognize you by smell and will realize
this is a handling event. Do not allow other pets near you when handling your corn. I have seen pictures of snakes seemingly lounging
with cats and dogs, but do not presume your snake will react favorably
to such household pets.

If the corn constantly evades being picked up or acts aggressively,
consider wearing gloves. Do not use gloves made of leather as the
smell could be perceived as that of a predator and could elicit a bite.
Of course, it won't hurt you to be bitten through the glove, but your
corn could lose teeth in the process. Another way of avoiding bites
from non co-operative corns is to gently lay a hand towel over the
snake before grasping it. If the towel is covering the head of the
snake, it is less likely to bite, but you should still grasp the snake in the
middle of the body. Once you have the snake out of the cage, you can
remove the towel and there should be no further aggressive behavior.

Where to Acquire Captive-Bred Corns

If you are considering the purchase of a corn snake based on pictures
you've seen, be prepared for a bit of a shock. Corns are one of the
most metamorphic (*transforming*) of all snake species in terms of
color and sometimes pattern. Most pictures of corns you find in books
and on the Internet are those of adults. Because neonate corns look
very different from their adult counterparts (usually less colorful), sometimes it's difficult to envision that a young one will mature to be like the
pictures that attracted you to the corn morph you're considering. If you
like the colors you see in a neonate corn, you'll love the way it will
mature. They always get better with age.

Pet Stores

As recently as the 1960s, the only corns available were the various
colors of the classic wild type pattern. Bear in mind that this was
before the Information Highway (*The Internet*) so the hobby then was
nothing like we know it today. The majority of corn snake owners
were individuals that lived in states where corns could be captured

---

The Reverse Okeetee corn snake is one of the most beautiful morphs being offered by breeders.

outdoors. I seldom saw them in pet shops in the Midwest and about the only knowledge the pet store owners had about them was their docile nature and their fondness for eating mice. Most of those pet shop owners did not even know they should be maintained above room temperature. There was little or no data published about caring for corns at that time.

Today, it is an entirely different market. Increasingly more pet stores are selling reptiles and doing a good job of it. Virtually all U.S. pet stores are governed by state or municipal agencies that perform frequent inspections to monitor compliance with animal welfare regulations. Buying from a pet store where you can see and hold the corn snake before purchase has an advantage over buying one sight-unseen, but pet shops often do not know the gender and genetics of their snakes.

Some questions to consider asking the sales attendant include:

* How long has this snake been in your store?
* How old is this snake? (Don't be alarmed if they do not know)

* Are you aware of any health issues affecting this snake?
* What and how often have you been feeding it?
* Is this a male or a female?
* What guarantee do you have regarding its health?

It is also advisable to get a business card from that pet store and have the attendant put his or her name on the back. Save your sales receipt as proof of when you purchased the snake.

After reading the **DISEASES AND DISORDERS** chapter, you'll know more about the outward physical signs of good vs. poor health. At a pet store, you also have the opportunity to personally evaluate the snake's temperament before buying. After your purchase, it is a good idea to procure the services of a snake breeder or qualified reptile veterinarian to get a second opinion on the proper gender of the snake and to at least get a general evaluation of its health.

Be careful on the trip home. It doesn't have to be mid-summer for a snake to die from overheating in the car. I know of situations where new corn snake owners held their snake near the car heater on the way home to keep it from getting too cold, only to find it dead in the container when they got to their destination. Likewise, the extreme cold from your car's air conditioner is dangerous. Precondition your car for median temperatures before taking your snake home. Avoid exposing it to sunlight for more than a few minutes at a time. If inside a clear or opaque container, snakes are especially susceptible to the "greenhouse effect" by the build up of heat that cannot adequately vent out. Plan your excursion so you make no unnecessary stops along the way.

The Internet

This is the fastest way to find corn snake breeders. The first suggestion I have if you're considering an Internet purchase is to frequent one or more of the chat forums specifically designed for corn snake discussions. Some of these sites will be listed in the back of this book. By conversing with other corn snake owners, you'll gain insights and information that could be crucial in successfully acquiring a healthy corn.

Questions you should ask in the chat forums include:

* What breeders or pet stores are or are not reputable?
* What kind of corn should I get?
* What type of cage should I use?
* Where can I buy frozen rodents?
* When is the next reptile expo in my area?

When you speak to the Internet seller you're considering, ask the following questions:

* How long has this web site been in operation?
* Do you have a written warranty?
* How old is this snake?
* Did you produce this snake? If not, who did?
* What have you been feeding it and how often?
* Are there any health issues of which I should be aware?
* Do you guarantee correct gender?
* What is the genetic background of the snake?
* How do you pack and ship your snakes and do you guarantee live delivery? (Avoid doing business with sellers that do not guarantee live delivery.)

Reptile Expos

Here is another opportunity to see before you buy. One distinct advantage you have in attending a reptile expo is being able to ask questions to the person that hatched the snakes. Because you have the opportunity to speak directly to the breeder, you potentially gain an essential genetic background on the snake(s) you're considering. Sometimes, when you are buying from a person that is reselling a snake, you don't get accurate, first-hand information regarding lineage.

The top shows in the country include the National Reptile Breeders Expo in Florida and the North American Reptile Breeders Conferences in Anaheim, Chicago, and Dallas.

Most breeders at the shows are proficient in determining the sex of the snakes so they are usually your best source in avoiding potential future breeding disappointments. There's little in our hobby more disappointing than investing three years of food, labor, and time into a snake only to find out it isn't the gender you thought you were buying. If your corn is just a pet, such a mistake probably will not matter, but if you had breeding plans for that snake, those plans could be jeopardized by misidentification. Even the breeders make mistakes, but if he or she is experienced and has a good reputation in the industry, you are less likely to encounter this particular disappointment. Unlike most pet stores that don't even know the gender of the corns they sell, most breeders actually guarantee you'll receive the gender you ordered.

If you purchase animals at a reptile expo, be sure to get a business card from the seller. Be leery of any vendor that does not offer business cards or is otherwise reluctant to give you contact information. This is sometimes a sign that they have fraudulent reasons for not wanting you to contact them after the sale. Always get a receipt from the seller with his/her name and contact information. Hopefully this won't be necessary, but in the event of a problem, you'll be glad you have it. There is often no recourse if you end up with a sick or dead corn snake you bought from someone that did not offer a warranty. Generally speaking, corn snake breeders that depend on reptile sales as their primary income are the ones most likely to ensure your satisfaction.

Chapter TWO: HOUSING

Ten-gallon terrariums make ideal cages for young corn snakes.

Before discussing the details of housing and caging, it must be emphasized here that the most essential prerequisite for keeping corns healthy is providing adequate **HEAT**. I emphasize that word because without proper heat, your corn will eventually get sick and die.

Housing Supplies List

Before acquiring your new corn snake, be sure to set up and test your enclosure and accessories. Here is your shopping list. Details for each item will follow the list.

* Cage with secure cover or door
* Heating device(s)
* Thermostat or rheostat (both optional)
* Hides (hiding places)
* Thermometers (two or more recommended)
* Hygrometer (optional)
* Water bowl
* Substrate (aspen recommended)
* Lighting (optional)

Platic "habitat" cages are ideally sized for young corn snakes, but difficult to heat.

Keep in mind that the pet industry is not regulated by agencies such as the FDA *(Food and Drug Administration)*. You will often find a picture of a corn snake on the package of a product that is considered unsafe or actually toxic to corns. These manufactures may be unaware of the dangers of using such products so you should research which products are safe and which should be avoided prior to shopping for your corn snake cage and accessories.

Cage (with secure cover or door)

Corns have roughly 1/5 the metabolism of mammals and therefore require relatively little exercise. Routine handling is usually sufficient. Consequently, their cages don't need to be spacious. In fact, small cages are more easily and economically heated than large ones. A corn snake cage that might be too small and has proper heating is better than a spacious cage with inadequate heating.

Most corn snake owners use fish aquariums constructed of glass. For hatchling corns, a 10 gallon (38 liter) aquarium is an ideal size. This should accommodate your corn for the first one to two years. The most popular cages used for adult corns are 20-30 gallon (75-113 liter) aquariums. It is recommended that you keep just one corn snake per

Communal housing of corn snakes can lead to cannibalism.

cage. As adults, corns rarely cause injury to each other when communally housed, but neonates are at great risk when caged together.

Most breeders in the United States use plastic storage boxes to house their snakes. They are usually arranged in rack systems and either the entire room is heated or the racks have individual heating. The heat for these racks is under or behind each box. Some use lids for each box while others slide the boxes onto the shelves, utilizing the shelf above it to prevent escape. These caging systems are impractical for the casual corn snake keeper. If you only have a few corns, aquaria make the best cages. Storage boxes are not efficiently heated unless they are part of a rack system.

The preferred materials for the bottom and sides of a corn snake cage are glass, acrylic, or other nontoxic materials with smooth surfaces. This is important for maintaining cleanliness. The micro-porosity of surfaces such as wood can harbor germs and parasites even when coated with paints or lacquers. I do not recommend using paints or lacquers on any surface that comes into contact with your snake. Any coatings used on the cage or accessories must be allowed to cure for a duration at least twice the manufacturer's recommendations to ensure adequate curing. The heating device you use to warm your snake can promote slow curing of such coatings and cause the release of toxic fumes in the cage.

For proper ventilation, the most efficient closure for your aquarium is a screen lid. Many reptile accessory manufacturers

A rack system allows a keeper to house a large number of snakes in an efficient manner.

produce aquarium lids specifically designed for snakes. Most of these lids have nylon screen to reduce rust and corrosion from exposure to moisture. Any crevice or hole your snake can get its head into will also accommodate its body. Be sure the lid is securely seated around the top of the aquarium and that there are no rips in the screen. Some glass aquarium-type cages have metal or plastic framed nylon screen tops that slide into guides at the top of the cage. Do not underestimate the resourcefulness of your corn to find the only little place in the cage you forgot to seal. Being nocturnal, they have all night to fully explore their cage and will do so routinely. If there is a place from which to escape, they'll find and use it.

Do not position your corn's cage near an air conditioning or heating vent or near a window. Light coming through a window can create a "greenhouse effect" in the cage and temperature spikes could be deadly to your snake. Likewise, air conditioning and heating vents blowing into your cage can cause sometimes volatile temperature fluctuations that could adversely affect your pet's appetite and digestion. High traffic areas in your home are usually beneficial in getting your snake accustomed to commotion and vibrations.

Heating Devices

We mammals are endothermic (*warm blooded*). Our bodies create and maintain optimum metabolic temperatures. Like all snakes, corns

As corn snakes grow, they can be moved to larger and more elaborate enclosures. Courtesy of John Stolz / Tails -N- Scales, Derby Kansas.

are ectothermic (*cold blooded*). They are incapable of internally maintaining sufficient body temperature to facilitate digestion. A corn snake's body temperature is essentially the same as that of their immediate surroundings. This does not mean they thrive in low temperatures. When not brumating your snake *(a state of low temperature dormancy similar to hibernation)*, it should have access to a hide that is 80-85° F (27-29° C). Proper digestion is not possible at constantly lower temperatures. They can survive continually cool temperatures when brumating, during which time their lower body temperature results in a reduced expenditure of calories. In captivity, the brumation period should be as cold as possible within the range of 45-65° F (7-18° C). More brumation details will be outlined in the **BREEDING** chapter.

Most corn snake keepers cannot dedicate an entire room to their snake so heating cages individually is necessary. Regardless of what heating device you use, it's essential to offer your corn more than one thermal zone within the cage. Thermo-regulation is necessary for digestion. The snake will know when it needs heat and when it should be away from the heat, but it's very important to offer both zones. Therefore, be sure heating devices are associated with only one end of the cage. This is especially important in unexpected situations where the room

A reptile heat mat should be placed under one end of a corn snake's enclosure.

gets too warm. Without thermostats or rheostats, heating devices are fully ON all the time, regardless of room temperatures. If one end of the cage is not heated, your corn can retreat to that zone until you adjust the heat on the warm end accordingly.

Never use "hot rocks" or related devices for warming corns. These are ideal for some basking lizards, but snakes can suffer serious and sometimes life-threatening burns from being too near these rocks. There should always be a buffer between a snake and its heat source.

(UT) *Under Tank* Heaters

The safest and most efficient device for heating your corn is the UT (*under tank*) heater. Some are constructed of composite carbon strips that are laminated between two panels of plastic and wired in resistance configuration. Less energy is required for this heating device. Most UT heaters are rated for approximately 10 watts of electricity so they are very energy efficient and therefore more environmentally friendly than light bulbs. UT heaters do not have flimsy filaments like light bulbs so they rarely need replacement.

To maximize the efficiency of the UT heater, you should install it under a glass-bottom cage. If your UT heater is one without an adhesive surface for applying to glass, use a strong fiber-reinforced tape, overlapping all four edges. Apply securely to the bottom surface of the glass toward one end of the cage. Since your snake also requires cooler temperatures to facilitate thermoregulation, you should never heat

A commercially available heat mat. Photo by Edison Gabrintina.

the entire bottom of the cage. UT heaters should be no larger than 25-33% of the length of your cage. Applying the UT heater to a side of the cage would essentially be worthless in adequately warming your snake. Most of the heat would be outside the cage and since hot air rises, virtually no heat would reach your snake.

When using self-adhesive UT heating pads, it is recommended that you also overlap the edges with tape for reinforcement. Periodic inspection of the UT heater is recommended to ensure that it is functioning properly and always in contact with the bottom of your cage. Once self-adhesive pads are attached to a surface, they cannot be removed or damage may result. Do not use UT heaters inside the cage. The cord could interfere with closing the lid and the wiring of these heaters is not always waterproof.

I do not recommend attaching UT heaters to any surface other than glass. There have been cases of warping and cracking damage to acrylic and other plastics. It is even possible to melt plastics with a UT heater. Operating UT heaters in empty cages has been known to crack glass, but such occurrences are rare. An adequate substrate draws heat away from the glass which usually prevents overheating and subsequent damage. I always recommend a one to two inch substrate depth (2.5-5 cm) of aspen bedding. Newspaper and paper towels should not be used with UT heaters. Many layers would be required to create the necessary buffer between the snake and the hot glass. Shredded newspaper should never be used. Never apply UT heaters to wood, cardboard, fabric or variations thereof. Such combustible materials are fire hazards when in direct contact with this degree of heat. Be sure there is air space between the UT heater and the surface beneath your cage. Fish aquariums are built with such an air space and are ideal for use with UT heaters.

Caution: The heat from a UT heater is capable of drying out or even burning a combustible material beneath it. I have seen the tops of wood furniture ruined by the heat below the UT heaters. It is therefore recommended that you set the cage on sturdy blocks or other devices that will increase the air space beneath the cage. Do not place fabrics such as towels or carpet in the air space where they might come into contact with the heater.

Lights and Heat Emitters

There are situations where OT (*over tank*) lighting or heat emitters are necessary, but for corn snakes, those situations are rare. Sometimes your cage is in a location too cool for the UT heater to efficiently heat. If your corn is sufficiently warmed by the UT heater but the air space in the cage above the snake is too cool, OT heat may be warranted. In those situations, use of a low wattage light bulb or heat emitter to warm the air in the cage is acceptable. Light bulbs and heat emitters should be installed in dome-like reflective fixtures that can be secured to the lid of your cage. Dogs and cats have been known to knock lights off the tops of cages. Not securing the light properly could create a serious fire hazard.

Note: Any OT heating device should be located on one end of the cage only. The other end should always be cool so your corn will have a retreat if overheating occurs.

I recommend that you do not depend on OT lights or heat emitters for raising your snake's body temperature, but if you do decide to use OT heating as a primary heat source, here are some tips to maximize efficiency. Most light bulbs are very fragile. If they don't shatter from being dropped or roughly handled, the filament in them often breaks. Heat emitters are initially more expensive, but do not have the flimsy filaments of light bulbs. Both use considerably more electricity than UT heaters and since hot air rises, most of the heat from OT heating never reaches your snake. In cases where your corn is not warm enough from OT heating, consider covering part of the screen lid near the light with non-flammable panels. This will restrict airflow and trap some of the heat that was formerly venting through the open screen. Be careful not to let anything covering part of the screen come into contact with the bulb, emitter or fixture. Also, spot lights are more efficient than standard light bulbs by directing light and heat to one place in the cage.

Thermostats or Rheostats (both optional)

Either of these temperature-controlling devices can be efficient and convenient for managing temperatures in your snake's cage. Thermostats can be set to control the temperature of the cage automatically. Rheostats (*dimmer switches*) can be manually adjusted for similar results, but require constant monitoring when room temperatures fluctuate. Sometimes using both of these devices simultaneously offers an adjustable temperature that is automatically cycled. If either or both of these control devices are employed, daily monitoring of correctly located thermometers is still recommended. Electrical switches of any kind are not made to last forever and if one of these devices failed in the open position, the resulting uncontrolled heat could kill your pet.

Hides (Hiding Places)

Corns are generally crepuscular (*active at twilight*), but in captivity, corns are most active in the dark. Therefore, during the daylight hours, corns like to be hidden. While they are quite capable of adjusting to bright-light situations, they prefer darkness. Perhaps their instincts are geared toward the concept that they are less qualified to evade diurnal *(active during daytime)* predators than those at night. Whatever the reasons are, corns not only appreciate their hides, but instincts often make them prisoners in them during the daylight hours. This is why it is recommended that you offer a hide on the warm end, the cool end, and one other place in the cage. If the only place in the cage with the correct digesting temperatures is not hidden, they usually will not utilize it. Their instinct to hide during the day seems to be stronger than their instinct to maintain safe body temperatures. This can result in feeding problems for your corn. Hides do not have to be sophisticated or aesthetic. They can be as simple as a piece of bark, a small box, or a flower pot with an access hole. Even a clump of artificial

Natural looking hides are available in pet stores and from numerous online sources. Photo by Ryan Moss.

floral leaves in the corner offers your corn snake the privacy it seeks. Most live plants are safe to use provided the soil has no fertilizers, however, corns will usually burrow into the soil and scatter it throughout the cage. If using bark sections that are open at both ends, position them so as to eliminate as much light under them as possible. Just because a snake can get under a hide does not mean it is dark enough inside. Your corn will be less stressed when there are hides in the cage that are truly dark inside. Do not depend on your snake to burrow in the substrate to escape the light of day.

Thermometers/Hygrometers

Because temperature is such a critical factor in keeping your corn snake healthy, using more than one thermometer is recommended. Why chance such an important requirement to only one thermometer that may not be properly located or may not be functioning properly? Instructions for most thermometers include a diagram showing where they should be located in the cage. Unfortunately, most of those show the thermometer on an inside wall of the cage. Since the temperature on the back glass of a vivarium can be as much as 15 degrees warmer or cooler than hides on the floor of the cage, thermometers are essentially useless above your snake. Whether you do or don't comply with the manufacturer's recommendations, know the reason for having a thermometer in a corn snake cage. It is not to know the temperature on the glass six inches above the snake's head. You must know the temperature of the snake. Since corns are ectothermic, you discover their body temperature by knowing the temperature next to them. Your corn is not likely to sit still while you put a thermometer against its body so the next best thing is to know the temperatures in the critical thermal zones within the cage. The two main zones are INSIDE the hides on both ends of the cage. If you have provided an adequately warm hide on one end, your corn should be spending most of its daytime hours in it. If it's too warm or too cool in that hide, your snake will not stay there. Regardless, you should know the temperature INSIDE both hides. The danger of the warm hide not being used by your snake is that it will be spending too much time in temperate zones not adequate to facilitate digestion. This is very dangerous. Of course, the only way to discover the temperature within these hides is by placing thermometers inside them. Not outside those hides. The thermometers do not need to remain in the hides at all times. If you have only one thermometer, occasionally set it next to a thermometer elsewhere in the house for comparison. One that you know works properly. Both should indicate the same temperature, plus or minus two degrees Fahrenheit. If you have just one thermometer and it's functioning properly, a second one is not necessary. However, having a back-up for emergencies is a wise precaution. Your goals are 80-85° F (27-29° C) inside the warm hide and below 80° F (27° C) inside the cool hide. The temperature on the cool side of the cage will vary depending on the time of day and temperature of the room. This is acceptable, provided the warm hide is always between 80° F and 85° F (27-29° C). Even if a third hide is nothing more than artificial flora, it would be wisely positioned between the warm and cool ends.

Corns tolerate a wide range of ambient humidity in their cages. For this reason, it is rarely necessary to monitor humidity levels in the cage. If you do use a hygrometer, ambient humidity levels of 15% to 90% are generally acceptable. One indication of inadequate ambient humidity is when your snake sheds its skin in multiple pieces instead of one or two long sections. One way of altering ambient humidity in the cage is by manipulating the volume of the water bowl. More details are outlined in the **SHEDDING** chapter later in the book.

Water Bowl

Corns do not necessarily need to have a water bowl large enough to submerge in, but they do sometimes enjoy soaking. The bowl doesn't

There is a wide variety of water bowls available for corn snake keepers. Photo by Ryan Moss.

need to be new, but should be thoroughly cleaned and sanitized if it was previously used for other purposes. The composition of the bowl is also unimportant as long as it holds water and is not made of a material that will contaminate the water. Water bowls that are light colored will sometimes aid in the detection of potential health threats. If corns have ectoparasites such as ticks or mites, they often instinctively soak in their water. Since most snake parasites are dark colored, any parasites that drown as a result of your corn soaking will be more easily detected in light colored water bowls.

The location of the water bowl is not crucial, but if it is too close to the heat source, the water may evaporate too quickly. Change the water twice a week or whenever you notice it is not clean. The type of water to use will be detailed in the **FEEDING AND WATERING** chapter.

Substrate

The safest and most efficient substrate beddings to use are wood pulp products other than cedar. Such absorbent substrates quickly desiccate moisture from feces and spilled water. Without moisture, bacteria cannot thrive. This not only reduces germ levels in the cage, but helps eliminate odors. Another benefit from using wood bedding products is their natural tendency to consolidate fecal masses. Sometimes just hours after your corn defecates, the stool can be removed in a small clump for convenient disposal. Spot cleaning like this means you often only need to completely change the substrate every two or three months. Most corn snake breeders use aspen bedding. After using most of the other substrate materials in the industry, I would not use anything else. Aspen is the most neutral smelling of the wood pulp products and I find its shape and color to be the most aesthetic. It contains the least amount of dust of any natural wood products I've used. Most grades of aspen accommodate burrowing when the snake wants to be closer to the UT heat source. The matting effect of most grades of aspen also makes it easy to alter the substrate surface temperature simply by increasing or reducing its depth.

There are at least four substrate materials you should never use for corn snakes. Never use sand, gravel, cedar or tree bark products. Sand and gravel have no absorption properties. In sand and gravel, when water is spilled or your snake defecates on it, the moisture is trapped in the substrate where it becomes a growth medium for bacteria and other germs. It will eventually evaporate, but the interim bacterial growth will contribute to odors and poor hygiene for your snake. Cases of intestinal impaction have been attributed to sand consumption. Cedar is toxic to your snake and prolonged exposure to it will cause nerve damage that can result in death. I have seen cases where a snake died the same day cedar was introduced to the cage. The bark of trees contains the highest concentrations of harmful chemicals. One piece of bark in the snake's water could pollute it with harmful chemicals that will be consumed by your pet during its next drink. Also, if ingested, the relatively large sizes of bark pieces are not easily passed through the digestive tract.

Another organic substrate that is not safe for corns is ground nut shells. While the shells of nuts are indigestible and allegedly benign when ingested, most shell fragments have very sharp edges. By virtue of not being digested, the sharp-edged pieces pass through the intestines and can have a lacerating effect, not unlike broken glass. Nut shell pieces are barely absorbent so I can see no reason to use this product as a cage substrate for your corn snake.

Sheet newspaper and paper towels are used by some breeders. These work well if you are heating the entire room, but if you individually heat

Many safe substrate materials for corns are available at pet stores. Photo by Ryan Moss.

cages with UT or OT heating, these paper products can prove to be dangerous to your snake. In the case of UT heaters, this allows the snakes to get too close to the heat. When using OT heating, there is no buffering substrate under which the snake can burrow to escape the heat above. An inadequate buffer such as sheet paper often results in over heating of the cage floor and sometimes sores from burns can result in secondary infections. Spilled water and feces tend to be held by the newspaper too long before evaporating. Snakes are often lying on feces-dampened paper for hours at a time. Such spills on aspen bedding tend to be isolated and do not spread as much as those on paper. Superior to paper, on aspen, the snakes are able to lie on the upper substrate levels that dried quickly from the air.

Other commonly used safe substrates include:

Shredded coconut husk, compressed and pelleted paper, peat moss and potting soil that does not contain fertilizer. Some of the moss products can temporarily color stain your snake's skin, but are not considered toxic. Artificial grass mats or outdoor carpets are other floor covering options. The primary problem with these mats is their propensity to hold liquids and smells.

Lighting (optional)

In captivity, even for nocturnal species, there is nothing wrong with a daytime photo period for your corn. Obviously, anything living above ground is exposed to daylight for part of most days, whether or not it elects to utilize it. While corns will benefit from cage lighting by way of experiencing day/night cycles, they do not require UVB radiation for efficient metabolism like most diurnal species. Indirect exposure to light from windows or ceiling lights in the room is sufficient to represent photo periods. This observation is from personally having healthy, breeding corns for over 30 years without individual cage lighting.

Cage Cleaning

If you are using a previously occupied cage, be sure it has been thoroughly cleaned and disinfected prior to use. If you spot clean by removing stools routinely, you can go weeks or even months without completely cleaning your corn's cage. When you decide to do a complete cleaning, here are some guidelines.

Put your corn in a safe place while cleaning the cage. Not only safe for the snake in terms of being out of the reach of the family cat or dog, but in a place where it's not too hot or cold. Pillow cases are convenient, but use old ones since snakes often defecate in unfamiliar surroundings. Check the pillow case for secure seams before using it and be sure the snake's head is a safe distance when knotting it closed.

Caution: If you set your snake down outside a cage, do not turn your back to it. Corns are cunning and almost seem to know when you're not looking. I get many phone calls and emails annually from snake keepers whose corns escaped from being out of their sight for only seconds.

There are detergents and germicides marketed specifically for cleaning animal cages, but most common household cleansers and disinfectants are adequate. If your hot water is over 180° F (82° C), contact for over ten minutes is usually sufficient to kill most bacteria. If you are using laundry or dish detergents, be sure they are in contact with all surfaces of the cage for at least ten minutes. The same applies to using bleach or ammonia. Mix one capful of bleach per gallon of cool water or mix one part ammonia to ten parts water for proper disinfecting strengths. A minimum of ten minutes is required to soak into the micro-

Large enclosures make wonderful homes for pet corn snakes even though they require more work to keep clean. Note the location of temperature and humidity monitors inside the hides where corns spend most of their time. Photo by Laurie and Jerry Spicher.

porosity of all surfaces in and on the cage. PineSol® and Lysol® brand products have proven to be lethal to snakes. Avoid using these products in the vicinity of snakes and their cages. Rinse all surfaces with hot water. Dry with clean towels or allow the cage to air dry completely. Never use air fresheners around your corns. Many contain chemicals that are known to kill snakes. Clean cage fixtures in the same manner and dry completely before returning them to the cage.

Note: Corn snakes are territorial by nature. For scenting purposes, it's not uncommon for them to defecate soon after being placed into a new or freshly cleaned cage. This usually occurs within the first hour so be ready to clean a mess shortly after introduction to the cage.

Chapter THREE: RECEIVING YOUR CORN SNAKE

Before receiving your corn snake, be sure to procure a supply of adequately sized prey. See the **FEEDING AND WATERING** chapter for details. Your cage should be set up and heating prior to acquiring your corn snake. Hopefully you cannot find any escape openings and the temperatures are stable. The last item to install in the cage is your corn snake.

If you are bringing your snake home from a reptile expo or pet store, you've already inspected it prior to purchase. You may now introduce it to the cage you have prepared. Do not handle it or allow too much commotion near the cage for the first 24 to 48 hours. This acclimation period is important for territorial animals like corns.

If you ordered your corn snake Online and it was shipped to you, here is what you can expect upon delivery of your new pet:

At the time of this writing, it is not legal to ship snakes via the United States Postal Service. Therefore, you are probably receiving your snake through one of the door-to-door carriers or will pick it up at the airport from one of the airlines that allow reptile shipping.

Ensure that someone is prepared to receive the package if it is to be delivered to a home or business. The majority of door-to-door deliveries arrive before noon the day after shipping, but if you're located outside their nearest delivery zones, the package could arrive in the afternoon or even early in the evening. Reasons for late-day deliveries include holiday traffic, bad weather, and vehicle malfunctions. In rare cases, your new snake could even arrive the second day after shipping. Most snake shippers pack for such eventualities and it's rare for animals that were properly packed to arrive dead, even when shipping complications result in severe delays.

Most reptile sellers will not guarantee live delivery unless the first delivery attempt is successful. In the event that someone is not available to accept delivery, the carrier will either leave it outside your door or put it back on their truck to be delivered later. This sometimes means the snake remains on the truck for many hours or for the rest of the day. Often, in cases of delivery exception, a second attempt is not made until the following day so it's important to have someone available to accept the package all day when you are expecting delivery.

Upon receiving your new corn snake, remove it from the shipping box. Hatchlings and sub adults are usually shipped in plastic containers with ventilation holes.

Larger corns are sometimes shipped in cloth bags. At this

Young corns are usually shipped in ventilated plastic cups, surrounded by insulation and heat or cold packs.

point, you can remove the snake and inspect it for injuries or other health aspects. Consider keeping (and not immediately cleaning) the shipping container or bag. Often in new surroundings, corns will be reluctant to feed. The cup or bag has familiar "home" smells and will help them acclimate to their new surroundings when placed inside the cage.

It is a good idea to inspect your new corn snake the same day it arrives. Most breeders require that you contact them immediately upon delivery if you discover anything wrong with the snake. You should at least inspect for:

* Normal locomotion
* Rapid and frequent tongue activity
* Firm muscle tone
* Parasites
* Any obvious injuries or anatomical abnormalities

If no problems are detected, let your new corn get settled in for a few days before beginning routine handling. Most corns are delivered feeling cold to the touch. Do not warm them quickly. Allow them to reach cage temperature gradually. Likewise, if overheated, do not shock them with cold air or water. If there is a qualified reptile veterinarian near you, considering having them examine your new pet. Get references from other corn snake keepers for the best reptile veterinarian near you.

Note: Quarantine your new pet. If you have other snakes, it is advisable not to expose them to your new arrival for many weeks. While most captive-bred snakes today are relatively free of diseases and parasites, it's not safe to presume this one won't possess a problem it can transmit to your other pets. The new snake should be housed in a separate cage as far away from other reptiles as possible. A different room is recommended. Do not cross handle from one snake to another without thoroughly washing your hands and arms first. Diseases and parasites can also be transmitted from clothing, so for the first 30 days or more, try to make your new snake the last pet you handle for that day. By the following day, you have bathed or showered and are wearing a change of clothing so you know you are not transmitting any germs to your other snakes via your skin or clothing. 30 days is a minimum quarantine period for health observation and I recommend at least 60 days.

Sometimes corns are nervous and it's not rare for them to display aggressive behavior for the first few days. They are not mentally capable of understanding why they were just exposed to all the motion and jostling of shipping so they are understandably confused. All the unfamiliar movement, noises, darkness, and smells from shipping and their new surroundings are enough to cause defensive and sometimes aggressive behavior. This is one of the most likely times you could be bitten by your corn. For this reason, when you take the shipping container out of the box, you may want to set it inside the cage before opening it. Let the snake emerge from the shipping container on its own. This could happen quickly or it could take hours. Don't forget to close the cage. Investigation of the cage by your new pet is normal, but you do not want it inspecting the entire house because you forgot to secure the lid or door of the cage.

Being territorial, corns are sometimes shy to explore their new cage. This could result in dehydration and it's important that your snake drinks water as soon as it arrives. Upon receiving your new pet, gently place it inside the water bowl. Each time you handle it for the next week, put it directly in the water. Since corns tend to follow the walls of the cage at night, place the water bowl against one of the sides of the cage for the first few weeks so it's sure to get all the water it wants to drink. As an added precaution against dehydration, consider putting a bottle cap of water inside the hide where your new corn spends most of its time. The days are long and many nocturnal species only emerge from their hides at night. Use only pure drinking water for hatchling corns. More details about water are in the **FEEDING AND WATERING** chapter.

I recommend that you wait a few days before feeding your new corn. Most snakes are shipped with empty stomachs so you can expect that your new corn was last fed at least three days prior to shipping. Therefore, unless it shows signs of shedding, wait three or four days before offering food. Longer in the case of an impending shed.

Chapter FOUR: FEEDING
AND WATERING

Okeetee corn snake eating a mouse.

Most corn snakes sold today are established feeders unless otherwise noted by the seller. Guidelines pertinent to problematic feeders will be detailed later in this chapter.

It is a good idea to keep a record of all events pertaining to your corn. Standard index cards are excellent for recording feeding, shedding, and health data. You can devise your own system for noting such entries as food refusals. I date the card for the food offering and then draw a line through it if the offering was declined. In this way, I don't attempt feeding again the following day under the presumption it was not offered food per schedule.

Diet

Corn snakes are carnivores. Young corns prefer lizards, but the bulk of their lifetime diet in the wild consists of rodents. The number one

Pantherophis guttatus											**869**
REC: (37) 8-14-04											
(2005)											
1/2	MP	3/12	LP	5/15	F	7/23	F	10/19	S	1-7	S
1/8	MP	3-16	LP	5-20	F	7/30	F	10-23	F	1-8	FF
1/13	MP	3/21	LP	5/26	F	8-6	S	10/30	F	1-13	FF
1-19	MP	3/26	LP	6-1	F	8-11	F	11/6	F	1-21	FF
1/29	S	4/3	LP	6/12	S	8-18	F	11-13	F	1/27	H3
2/2	MP	4-10	S	6-18	F	8/26	F	11-25	S	2/9	S
2/8	MP	4/12	LP	6-24	F	9-4	F	11-27	F	2-11	H
2/14	MP	4-18	LP	6/30	F	9-12	S	12-1	F	2/18	H
2/20	LP	4-21	LP	7-09	S	9-18	F	12/7	F	2/24	H
2/26	MP	4-30	LP	7/11	F	4-24	F	12/14	F	2-30	H
3/5	S	5/8	S	7/16	LP LP	10-1	F	12-21	FF	3-7	FH
3/6	MP	5-10	LP	7-22	F	10/9	F	12-27	F	3/9	H

Data card legend for corn female number 869: mp = medium pinky, s = shed, lp = large pinky, f = fuzzy, h = hopper

food choice for corn snakes in captivity is mice. Except for occasions when young corns are preliminarily reluctant to eat rodents, many captive-bred corns go their entire lives having eaten nothing but mice. Being omnivores, we humans need a varied diet to satisfy our nutritional requirements. Corns get all the nutrition they need from eating rodents.

Like all snakes, corns are opportunistic feeders. In the wild, meals are sometimes few and far between so when hungry, corns rarely refuse any prey they encounter. Given the opportunity, and in the absence of their favorite prey (lizards, rodents, and birds), wild corns consume frogs, toads, salamanders, snakes, and even insects. There are many complications associated with feeding insects to corns in captivity so I never recommend it. Crickets and meal worms are probably the most dangerous insects to feed corns. Not only have those insects been known to kill snakes by biting them, but some young corns have died from internal injuries after ingesting them.

Rodents

Virtually all breeders and most hobbyists feed nothing but rodents to their corns. Mice are the most popular choice due to their convenient size. Some feed rats, but not only are the sizes of rats less convenient, they are also more expensive than mice. Feeding a steady diet of immature rats makes corns grow more quickly, but this is not necessarily beneficial to the overall welfare of the snake. Since the bulk of a corn snake's diet in the wild is mice, it makes sense to emulate that diet in captivity.

Wild animals should only be fed to your corn as a last resort. The risk of introducing parasites or toxins is great so why take the chance unless your snake refuses to eat anything else? That wild mouse you consider feeding your corn might have recently eaten rat poison in your neighbor's garage so you should not risk killing your snake for the sake of a free meal. Wild rodents are even more opportunistic than snakes when it comes to feeding. They will eat almost anything. In their foraging, they regularly ingest parasites and some of these parasites can complete their life cycles inside your corn, causing serious problems and even death.

By contrast, most rodents sold in our industry are not only relatively free of parasites, but have been fed scientifically balanced diets to ensure optimum nutrition for your snake. Commercial rodent breeders know that feeding only the highest quality foods to their mice and rats results in a better product for your snake. Avoid buying rodents from breeders that feed commercial dog foods to their mice and rats. This is not considered a proper diet so feeding those rodents to your corn can result in nutritional imbalances. Corns can subsist solely on rodents so a well-fed mouse or rat has sufficient vitamins and minerals to sustain them.

Gerbils and hamsters are also commercially available and have the same basic nutritional values as mice and rats. Gerbils and hamsters are much more aggressive and capable of injuring a corn so I recommend only feeding pre-killed gerbils and hamsters to your corns.

There are many companies that ship frozen rodents across the United States. You can order from your computer or by telephone and they're shipped in dry ice packaging. Most of these companies humanely kill the rodents and vacuum pack them to prolong frozen storage limits. One advantage of ordering Online is that you get the exact size you need, however pet stores that specialize in reptiles usually have a large variety of live and frozen rodents in stock.

A small Lavender corn snake feeding on a thawed pinky mouse.

No matter what type of rodent you choose to feed your corn, feeding them to your snake alive is not recommended. If you're not feeding thawed/frozen rodents, pre-killed ones will suffice. A common myth is that snakes will only eat live prey. This is generally untrue and the advantages of feeding dead prey to your snakes vastly outweigh the risks of feeding live prey. It is rare for live rodents to injure snakes in captive feeding events, but why risk injury or death to your pet unnecessarily? If you do feed live rodents to your corn, it's advisable to monitor such feedings and never leave the snake and rodent together without supervision. If improperly constricted, a live rodent can bite one or both of your snake's eyes. Snakes have relatively tough scales to protect them from sharp objects, but their eyes have no such protection. Damage from a bite could cause the loss of sight and sometimes results in the snake's death. Of course, neonatal mice don't have teeth and therefore do not present a biting danger. Corn snakes have one basic defense strategy. If striking, biting, or hissing does not dissuade unwanted company, they flee. How can your corn escape the unwanted advances of a hungry or thirsty rodent when it's trapped inside its cage? A hungry mouse will follow the snake throughout the cage, chewing on its body. The tail is most commonly damaged since it is furthest from the menacing mouth of the snake. These rodents are often relentless and will not stop until their hunger or thirst is satisfied.

This satisfaction is often only achieved when the snake is dead from such attacks. A corn will not kill a rodent to defend itself. Unlike most carnivores, corns apparently only kill to eat.

If you prefer not to feed whole prey, processed foods are available at many pet stores. These frozen rodent substitutes are advertised as a complete diet for corns. Most of these products are similar in appearance to sausage and contain some or all parts of rendered animals. They're usually cylindrically shaped for maximum digestive efficiency and are available in several sizes to accommodate the growth stages of corns. Much research was invested to discover the nutritional requirements of snakes and consequently these products should completely satisfy a corn's dietary needs. If ingredients are not listed on the packaging, don't hesitate to ask the manufacturer for details regarding nutrition. Ask friends that have tried the products you are considering or query the Internet browsers for information and testimonials about them. Corn snake chat forums on the Internet are usually good places to get more opinions about these processed rodent substitutes.

Corns need all the essential vitamins and minerals found in whole prey. Avoid feeding parts of animals to your corn snake. For instance, I know keepers that occasionally feed their corns raw chicken wings or drum sticks. While there is a great deal of protein and calcium in these parts, they lack many of the other essential nutrients found in the organs of whole prey. Also, feeding raw chicken to any animal sometimes results in the introduction of bacteria such as *Salmonella*.

Vitamins and Minerals

If the rodents you feed your corn were maintained on a properly balanced diet, there is little or no need to augment the snake's diet with vitamins and/or minerals. As it is with all dietary supplements, proper amounts will benefit your pets, but too much can be a potentially serious health risk to any animal. If you decide to offer vitamins and/or minerals to your snake, do so sparingly and seldom. The only supplements I feed my corns are phosphorus-free calcium with Vitamin D3. Some manufacturers offer these together in one product. Only my females receive these supplements and only once or twice per year when they're producing eggs. I have never found it necessary to supplement the diets of my adult males or neonates. I have used RepCal®

brand for many years with no adverse affects, but I'm sure most of these products available in the industry are satisfactory. Phosphorus is a calcium binder and snakes get enough of it in their prey so as a general rule, the supplementation of phosphorus is not necessary. If you wish to use a multi-vitamin, there are many designed specifically for reptiles. It is wise to research which ones are best suited for nocturnal serpents before making your purchase.

Most of these products are sold as powders, but multi-vitamins are sometimes available in liquid form. Whichever kind you use, one of the most efficient ways to dose is by applying some to the posterior end of the prey item. For adult corns, I just dab the rump of a pre-killed mouse onto approximately ¼ teaspoon of the powder that was sprinkled on paper. Dipping the prey item into the container is not recommended as it can contaminate the remaining powder. Corns almost always eat a mouse head first so if you apply the supplement to the head, it may be rejected. Offer the mouse head-first and the corn will never know the powder is on the other end.

Note: Powdered vitamin and mineral products should be stored in the freezer. Many vitamins break down more quickly at higher temperatures.

Size of Prey

Proper prey size is very important. A general rule is not to feed any food item that is more than 1.5 times the mid-body girth of the snake. If continually feeding prey that is too small, it will not affect digestion but may slow your corn's growth. On the other hand, feeding items that are too large can be dangerous. Since corns can distend their bodies to accommodate large meals, they are capable of ingesting prey many times the size of their head. This does not mean they should eat prey that size. In fact, if a meal in their stomach decomposes faster than it can be digested, it will be regurgitated. Bacterial growth within the meal causes it to swell and the corn will have no choice but to eject it. Anytime a corn regurgitates a meal, it is potentially life threatening and you must not feed that snake again without first discovering and correcting what caused the regurgitation. Post-regurgitation therapy will be detailed in the **DISEASES AND DISORDERS** chapter.

There are many mouse suppliers around the world that produce and ship frozen rodents. Photo by Big Cheese Rodent Factory.

If faced with the choice of feeding two small prey items vs. a single large one, I recommend you always choose feeding two small ones. If you're attempting to accelerate growth in your corn, one option is to feed a single food item twice as often as you normally would. Otherwise two at a time will suffice if they're not too large. Generally speaking, adult corns rarely require rodents larger than adult mice.

There are many mouse suppliers around the world that produce and ship frozen rodents. Live shipping is cost prohibitive so most snake keepers order them frozen. Terminology for the different sizes varies from one company to another, but the sizes are generally the same.

The smallest rodent a newly hatched corn can consume is a small pinky mouse. Though it may not look possible, few hatchling corns are incapable of ingesting a one-day old pinky mouse. A commonly asked question is, "How do I know when my corn is ready to move up to the next prey size?". My response is, "24 hours after feeding your corn, if the bulge corresponding to the food item in the stomach is not clearly visible, you may graduate to the next prey size". If you still have inventory of the smaller items, you can feed two at a time before advancing to the next size.

Frozen mice and rats are safely stored for up to 12 months in most residential freezers. Freezers today have line driers that reduce moisture, thus decreasing the need for frequent defrosting. This results in moisture being extracted from the rodents in your freezer. Signs of this dehydration appear in the form of spots on the rodents that resemble sores. These areas of dehydration are called freezer burns. I have fed freezer burned mice to corns with no obvious negative effects, but the longer they are dehydrating, the less moisture and mineral content they have. Vacuum packing helps, but since plastic containers are micro-permeable, dehydration and resulting freezer burns are not completely eliminated. To extend the freezer life of rodents or any other foods, freeze them in water. The ice shell you create buffers them from most of the dehydration and essentially doubles or triples the freezer life of those products. I don't recommend refreezing rodents your corn did not eat. Uneaten rodents should be disposed of properly. Many municipalities have ordinances against animal disposal in landfills so I recommend you flush them in your toilet or bury them outside.

Feeding Frequency

Most breeders feed their neonate corns once every five to seven days. Under proper cage conditions, most snakes completely digest a nominally sized meal in three days and will defecate shortly thereafter. Some keepers consider it safe to feed again immediately after defecation of the previous meal, but that is a relatively aggressive feeding routine. Since a corn's growth is commensurate to its food intake, increased feedings will result in faster growth. A feeding regimen of one prey item every four days is considered aggressive feeding. Feeding every two to three days is called power feeding and is not recommended. Under nearly perfect conditions, a neonate corn will thrive from being power fed, but there is an increased chance of regurgitation if done improperly. The most common negative conditions for any feeding regimen are improper temperatures and/or inadequate thermo-regulation options.

Just like any animal, as a corn's growth rate slows, it requires fewer calories. Therefore, when your snake reaches approximately 36" long (90 cm), it is considered mature and you should discontinue accelerated feeding regimens. A mature male corn snake should not lose weight in a proper cage environment when fed one appropriately sized prey item every seven to 14 days. I feed most of my mature males every 10-14 days. If you notice any loss of weight from this regimen, consider feeding males one food item every seven days. Any more than this for adult males can result in obesity. Over-feeding adversely affects the breeding performance of male corns and can lead to heart disease.

Mature females require more calories than males. At proper temperatures, adult female corns should be fed one appropriately sized prey item every five to seven days and that is a satisfactory regimen for their entire lives. I don't recommend feeding a mature female corn less often than once every seven days. During breeding seasons, I feed my adult females one appropriately sized food item every five days. Mature corns should never be power fed.

You will discover that after feeding your corn, it will still want to eat more. This is because of their instinct to take advantage of potential windfall food supplies. Under ideal conditions, their stomachs are designed to accommodate more than one food item per feeding, but like our dogs, cats and even our children, it is unwise to feed corns more than they need just because they want it. It's up to you to know when to stop feeding your snakes. If you feed them as much as they want, I guarantee they will not be healthy and they will die much sooner than they would have if you had practiced good nutrition management. Obesity also reduces the chances for successful reproduction.

Feeding Procedures

If you are feeding frozen rodent substitute products to your corn, follow the manufacturer's thawing instructions. If you use frozen mice, there are several ways to thaw them. One is to run hot water on them. If you prefer to feed dry mice so cage litter is not as likely to stick to the fur and be ingested, place the mouse in a plastic bag or wrap it in cellophane prior to hot water thawing. If feeding on a clean surface that is free of substrate particles, some keepers prefer to feed mice wet so as to increase the moisture content of the meal. Frozen pinky mice usually thaw in two to five minutes under running hot water or approximately four to 10 minutes in standing hot water. Adult mice usually thaw to room temperature in seven to 15 minutes under running hot water or around 20-30 minutes in standing hot water. Thaw times vary depending on frozen condition and temperature of the water. Placing an adult mouse in a cup of water is like putting an ice cube in it so don't expect the water to stay hot. On the other hand, I do not recommend "par boiling" so watch the clock to avoid cooking the meal. Thawing at room temperature on a paper towel is another effective method. Pinky mice usually thaw at room temperature in 60 to 90 minutes and if you want to thaw adult mice at room temperature, you'll be waiting approximately three hours. Bacteria thrive inside these mice once the rodent's body temperature reaches approximately 80° F (27° C). The longer the thawing food items are exposed to this temperature, the more bacteria your snake will be ingesting. Thawing by microwave ovens can work, but I recommend you use the lowest setting possible. Mice will explode inside microwave ovens if allowed to heat too long. So that you don't discover the correct thawing time for mice the hard way, I do not recommend thawing with microwave ovens. The test for determining if a rodent is properly thawed is to bend your finger and push your knuckle against the stomach of the mouse. If the core of the rodent feels slightly cool, it's ready to feed. If it feels warm, it's too hot to feed to your snake. Your touch is generally 95° F (35° C) so if it feels warm, it's well over 100° F (38° C). It's better to serve them too cool than too warm.

It is recommended that you feed your corn some place other than its cage. If your snake never receives a meal in its cage, it is less likely to confuse a handling event as a meal offering. How you offer food to corns is not usually important. Some keepers place the meal into the feeding container and then introduce the snake. Others introduce the food item to the snake after it's in the feeding container. Most captive corns will eagerly eat anywhere. An empty plastic container or even a bag or cardboard box is ideal for feeding outside your corn's cage. While ingestion of small pieces of the substrate bedding is not considered dangerous, a wet rodent can become virtually coated when placed directly upon a particulate substrate. That much foreign debris ingested by your corn could be dangerous over time.

As a rule, most corns don't care what time of day they are fed. Since wild corns mainly feed at night, some captive snakes prefer food offerings around sunset or later. The nocturnal feeding preference is rare for corns in captivity, but if cage conditions are correct and your snake is not in some stage of ecdysis (*shedding*), you should make nighttime food offerings to reluctant feeders.

Most keepers feed thawed mice to their corn snakes from forceps or hemostats.

If presenting food to your snake with your fingers, be sure your hands have been thoroughly washed and rinsed. Offering a meal to your corn snake with bare hands is usually safe, but any snake can sometimes become confused and unintentionally bite your fingers. With most snakes, after accidentally biting their keeper's hand, constriction will follow. Fortunately, corns usually realize their mistake immediately and release. Sometimes the size of your hand (even if you're just holding the tail of a mouse) will cause the snake to be threatened by the offering. Most corns sense that if a potential meal appears to be too large, the risk of personal injury to them is not justified. Hence, most corn snake keepers use forceps or hemostats for food presentation. These utensils have a smaller profile and therefore do not intimidate the snake. I find 12" dressing forceps to be the best tool for feeding all sizes of corns. If you use the forceps to pick up objects other than food for your snake, be sure to disinfect them before and after each use. Chopsticks also work well as a feeding tool.

Even when feeding thawed/frozen rodents, corns often instinctively go through the unnecessary motions of killing their intended meal. Constriction prior to feeding is rare for hatchling corns unless the prey item is moving. They will even swallow pinky mice alive and kicking, all the way to the stomach. Corns usually swallow rodents head-first, but breach feeding is not uncommon and nothing to worry about. I've seen adult corns fold large mice in half while swallowing them sideways. If a prey item is too large or the snake has begun the swallowing process inefficiently, they'll usually back off and proceed from a more successful strategic starting point.

The majority of corn snakes' natural foods are social animals. Therefore, it is their instinct to presume that where they find one prey item, there will be more. Often after eating, corns will seem very nervous. Not unlike the frenzied feeding habits of sharks, after eating one or more items, corns are likely to seize the first thing that moves. Being opportunistic feeders, it isn't uncommon for a wild corn to consume an entire nest of rodents or birds at one feeding. Hence, your pet could misjudge your hand to be another rodent, so use caution when picking up the snake after it eats. Usually, as soon as you have the snake in your hands, it will realize the feeding event is finished and you will not be bitten. Provided your hands do not smell like rodents, that is. Corns will usually try to eat anything that even remotely smells like their customary prey.

After your corn eats, it will usually seek out a warm place to accelerate its metabolism and facilitate digestion. It's a good idea to keep handling to a minimum for this three day digestion period. Some snakes are more stressed at this time and will even eject a meal as a result of the excess motion from being handled. In the wild, it's not uncommon for a corn to puke a meal when confronted by a predator since they can move more quickly with an empty stomach. Follow standard post-regurgitation therapy procedures if your snake ever regurgitates a meal. See **DISEASES AND DISORDERS** chapter for details.

Reluctant Feeders

It is rare for a healthy adult corn maintained at proper temperatures to refuse food offerings except during the breeding season or if they are in some stage of shedding. However, newly acquired neonates sometimes require encouragement. Most breeders sell only corns that are voluntarily feeding on thawed/frozen mouse pinkies, but sometimes the change of environment causes them to refuse even their favorite foods.

Do not repeat food offerings more often than once every three days if initial attempts are unsuccessful. If your neonate corn refuses to eat after three such offerings, try some of the following tactics.

Night Feeding

Wait until after dark to offer food. Since corns have ancient nocturnal instincts, they sometimes prefer to eat at night.

Cup Feeding

Keep the cup or container in which the snake was shipped. Unless it is excessively dirty, do not wash the cup. Being territorial by nature, sometimes the only reason they are not feeding is because they don't feel "at home", so familiar smells are appreciated. Even if you have washed the cup, sometimes offering meals in cramped containers is successful. Covering the cup or container with a cloth so the snake is in darkness and not distracted by commotion also helps. If the prey item is not consumed in 30 minutes, consider leaving the snake and food together in the container overnight. Do not offer live prey in such containers. Be sure the temperature in the container is not allowed to exceed 85° F (29° C) or fall below 70° F (21° C) overnight. A small paper bag also works well for such offerings.

Motion

Sometimes, your corn just wants to see a prey item move. If you are feeding thawed/frozen rodents, consider "jiggling" the offering at the end of forceps or hemostats.

The Hunt

Reluctant feeders are sometimes confused when their "meal" suddenly appears in front of them. Leaving their food offering at the end of the cage opposite where they slept all day is sometimes prudent. Such offerings can be made on the lid of a deli cup to reduce substrate ingestion. Do not alert the snake to the presence of the offering. Let it discover the intended meal naturally after emerging from the hide.

Washing

Domestic rodents are not the most hygienic animals on the planet. For some reason, they have lost their instinct to be as clean as wild rodent species. As a result, when a corn rejects such offerings, it's not because it doesn't want a rodent, but because the offering doesn't smell like a rodent. Gently wash the pinky in mild soapy water and thoroughly rinse and dry it. This is an amazingly successful technique.

Live Prey

It is rare, but sometimes, the age-old instinct for wanting live prey is strong in some corns. If the breeder of the corn you acquired was feeding live pinkies, you may have difficulties feeding pre-killed ones. If all motion efforts were not successful, you may need to feed live pinkies to your new corn for awhile. It will eventually eat pre-killed ones so don't despair.

Braining

This technique is not for the squeamish. We do not know why, but sometimes reluctant feeders are attracted to the smell of a rodent's brain. If other tactics have failed, consider exposing the brain matter of the pinky. The simplest way is to pierce the top of the rodent's head with a sharp object. A pin or needle will usually do the job. If no brain matter exudes from the opening you make with a pin or needle, you may have to use the sharp corner of a razor blade.

Scenting

Since the natural prey of neonate corns in the wild is not newborn rodents, changing the scent of the intended meal to fool the snake is sometimes required. Rubbing a lizard on the skin of the intended meal is a very successful technique. Eventually, less and less lizard scent is necessary until eventually, your corn will eat the offerings without scenting.

Tease Feeding

Akin to the 'motion' suggestion above, movement is elemental in this

---

technique. If simulating movement was not successful, try irritating the snake with the offering. Gently slapping the intended meal against the side of the snake will sometimes elicit aggression. Often the snake repeatedly strikes at the aggressor (the pinky) and will sometimes co-incidentally seize it. This usually triggers a feeding response. Hold very still if this happens and the snake will usually swallow the pinky in a few minutes. It may be necessary to repeat this process several times before success is achieved.

Exercise

As you can see, corns do not get much exercise in captivity. Even if they slither around in their cage all night, they seldom significantly increase their heart rates. Breeders have had great success with reluctant feeders by forcing them to exercise. Apparently the resulting increase in metabolism can sometimes stimulate appetite. Let your snake repeatedly crawl from one of your hands to the other. Another way is to follow your corn around the room. Be careful. They can crawl under furniture in the blink of an eye. Food offerings shortly after such *work outs* are often productive.

Force-Feeding

This should only be considered as a last resort. Not only is it difficult to do safely and effectively, but it's very stressful to the snake. Due to the potential dangers associated with the technique of force-feeding, consult an experienced snake breeder for technical advice. Do not attempt force feeding without such guidance.

Watering

Water quality is just as important for your snake as it is for you. Perhaps more so when considering the relatively small size of your snake. Most city water providers add chemicals to kill bacteria and other germs. Chlorine is the most common additive and is found in the public drinking water of almost every city in the modern world. Fluoride is also added to the water in many cities. Your adult corns may not be adversely affected by these chemicals, but small corns certainly are. Trace amounts of chemicals in drinking water will not have much impact on an adult human, but those same small levels could be toxic or even

A Gold Dust corn snake drinking water.

lethal to your corn. Therefore, I do not consider city tap water to be safe for hatchling snakes and I also suggest not using it for adult snakes.

I have not used dechlorination chemicals that are commonly used for tropical fish, but I presume that if they are safe for animals as fragile as tropical fish, they should be safe for corns to drink. Check labels for any chemicals you add to water. If it is unsafe for human consumption, do not use it for your corn.

Filtration systems are effective for producing pure drinking water for your corn. They can be as simple as the ones you attach to a faucet or pitcher and as complex as the reverse osmosis systems that schools and hospitals use to filter water. I have had great success with the filters that attach directly to the faucet. Using water softening systems is not recommended. The salt and potassium used in those systems to counteract the minerals in hard water are not considered safe for snakes. If you have no way of filtering the water, buy bottled water at the store. Do not use distilled water. There are many essential minerals in water that distillation removes. Water marketed as Spring Water and Drinking Water are safe choices. They can be purchased economically by the gallon at most grocery stores. Rain water is not recommended as it can contain chemicals from automobile and industrial pollution.

The size of the water receptacle is not necessarily important. As long as your snake can drink from it, any size is adequate. Corns will sometimes soak in their water bowl when preparing to shed, attempting to self eliminate mites or ticks and sometimes if the cage gets too hot. Therefore, a bowl size large enough to accommodate your snake is recommended, but not mandatory. Larger bowls contribute to ambient humidity and the higher water volume in them also facilitates the dilution of germs. Do not use fountains or water falls in your corn's cage. The amount of ventilation necessary to prevent molds from growing in that excessively damp environment would make the cage impossible to properly heat.

Check water bowls daily or bi-daily. It's not uncommon for snakes to defecate in their water. It's equally common for them to drink that water after doing so. Hence, the more frequently you check the water, the better your chances of avoiding health problems. Some corn snake owners maintain two water receptacles per cage in case one gets fouled.

Never add water to your snake's drinking receptacles. Each time the water level gets low, clean the bowl before rewatering. It just takes a minute and since most biologic pathogens are water borne, clean water is your first line of defense against internal parasites and diseases.

Note: If you plan to be away from your corn for several days and nobody will be checking on it in your absence, it's a good idea to put one or two extra water bowls in the cage in case one spills or becomes fouled.

Another advantage of checking water bowls regularly is the opportunity to spot parasites such as mites. Since snakes instinctively soak their bodies in water to rid themselves of external parasites, you have the advantage of finding out quickly if your snake has parasites. Drowned mites appear as black dots in the bottom of the water bowl. They are easily identifiable with a magnifying glass.

Chapter FIVE: SHEDDING

An opaque corn snake in the days before shedding. Photo by Bill Love.

Unlike most animals, a snake's outer skin does not continually stretch to accommodate growth. It must be replaced by a new skin layer. Ecdysis (*shedding*) is the process whereby the old, outer skin is sloughed in favor of the new and more flexible skin that was forming beneath it. *My general reference to skin actually refers to both the skin and scales.* Snakes that eat more often, grow more quickly and therefore will shed more frequently. While shedding is generally recognized as a byproduct of growth, there are other reasons for the process of skin replacement. The normal day-to-day activities of a snake cause wear on the outer skin. Even older snakes that are no longer growing are still active and therefore still require outer skin replacements. The new skin layer is under perpetual development. Other than accommodating growth and wear, shedding of the old skin can occur between the normal shedding cycles for the following reasons:

* Injuries to skin and scales
* Ectoparasites such as mites or ticks
* Diseases or fungal growths that might penetrate the dermis

* Reproductive events
* Respiratory infections

Since the skin replacement mechanism seems to be hormonally stimulated, even medications can alter the shedding cycles.

Usually the snake will have an opaque or "milky" appearance in the days prior to the separation phase of this cycle. Besides an overall dull appearance, the eyes are noticeably blue or white for several days. It's not uncommon for your corn to spend a great deal of time soaking in its water bowl to help soften the old skin. During this time, the snake's vision is impaired and its general instinct is to distrust anything that moves. I recommend that you not only avoid handling corns during this time, but that you also forego feeding until shedding is complete. Some corns will have an appetite during the shedding cycle, but many simply will not eat during this time. Regurgitation sometimes results when a corn voluntarily eats during a shed so not offering food during this cycle is the safest action. A bulge in the snake during shedding can also complicate the removal of the dead skin. If food is completely digested near the end of a shedding cycle, your corn will likely not defecate until the skin comes off. It's not uncommon to see feces inside the shed skin. Do not be alarmed if you don't notice tongue activity during the final stages of shedding. As soon as the skin is sloughed, normal tongue action will resume. Occasionally, a whistling or popping sound can be heard during the shedding period. This is thought to be skin flaps that are incompletely dislodged, thereby causing noises when the snake exhales. The noises should cease after shedding, but if they don't, consult a reptile expert or a qualified reptile veterinarian. These could all be signs of URI (*upper respiratory infection*).

The separation process takes approximately eight to 12 days from when you first notice the opaque look to the physical shedding event. Approximately two days before sloughing the skin, the eyes appear clear again. This signifies that the separation of skins is complete, but sloughing will not occur immediately. Young corns can shed as often as every three weeks with aggressive feeding schedules, but the average shedding frequency is every four to six weeks with standard feeding practices. Do not worry if your snake does not adhere to this general schedule. Every snake is different and the time between sheds is influenced by many different stimuli. Don't expect shedding frequency to decrease with age. Most of my older adult males shed once a month throughout the summer, even though they are no longer growing.

The first skin separation points are the upper and lower lip flaps. By pushing their snout against objects in the cage, the skin peels off at the rostrum (*snout*) and the snake slowly slithers out of it. Usually, corns shed in one piece. Since the shed skin includes parts that are beneath the peripheries of the scales, the skin is always longer than the snake itself. It can be as much as 40% longer than the snake, so don't gauge your corn's size by the length of the sloughed skin.

Some keepers refer to their corns in the opaque stage of shedding as "being in the blue". Photo by Ryan Moss.

Caution: Never initiate the shedding process. If the dead skin comes off prematurely, the snake can suffer sores that are surely painful and will be visible for one to two shedding cycles.

Retained Skin

Dysecdysis is the term used for incorrect or incomplete shedding of the dead skin. If the cage is too dry or the snake's nutrition levels are below normal, the old skin may not slough off or may come off in many pieces. The main cause for this is an excessively dry cage ambiance. Especially in the winter when the air is drier from home heating systems. Since the dead skin is no longer an element of the snake's hydrating system, it is potentially dangerous to leave attached. These pieces have a desiccating affect by wicking moisture from your snake.

Incomplete shedding is often caused by excessively dry cage conditions.

This not only affects their looks, but the resulting dehydration can cause potentially serious visceral damage. In addition, retained skin pieces can harbor bacteria and invite fungal growth.

If your snake is not shedding in one piece, consider increasing the ambient humidity in the cage. This can be done in many ways. One way is to increase the diameter of the water bowl and put it directly over the UT or under the OT heat source. Spraying the snake with water does not help and can sometimes exacerbate the problem. Not unlike licking your lips which makes them more chapped, water on the skin of your snake can displace natural emollients, thereby contributing to dehydration. Spraying water on the substrate in your cage will increase ambient humidity, but too

Remove unshed dead skin pieces as soon as possible.

Damp sphagnum moss is the best substrate for incomplete shedding.

much can promote the growth of mold and mildew. Placing a towel or sheet of plastic over part of the screen top on the cage helps trap some of the evaporating moisture. Lights above the cage contributes to drying out the air around your corn so only use them if your primary heat source is inadequate. If you use OT lighting, do not let flammable materials come into contact with lights.

The best way to facilitate proper shedding is to offer your snake a hide with damp sphagnum moss. Wet paper towels do not work well as the snake tends to mat them on the bottom of the hide. The natural shape of moss maintains structure and allows the snake to burrow in it. This allows the dry dead skin to be in constant contact with the damp moss. If you don't want to wait for the snake to naturally rid itself of these pieces, you can soak it in water. Make sure the water used to soak the snake is not so deep the snake will drown. The container must have air holes. The temperature of the water should be as close to the cage temperature as possible. Remember your touch is approximately 95° F (35° C) so proper water temperature should feel slightly cool. Place the container on the substrate near (not directly over or under) the heat source for one or two hours. After soaking, hold a wet cloth or wear wet cotton gloves and let the snake slither through them. Most (if not all) of the dead skin will rub off. You likely will not know if you got all the pieces off until after a few hours or the next day when the dry skin will be more obvious again. You can remove these dry pieces by using masking or painter's tape. Do not use tapes with strong adhesives. Dab the tape on the dry skin pieces in the same way you would remove lint from a sweater. Don't use tape to remove skin more than one week after the shedding process began. Premature removal of the new skin in development beneath the outer layer can result in potentially serious sores.

If the spectacle lenses (*eye caps*) did not come off with the rest of the soughed skin, tape should remove them from the eyes. The only sure way to know if eye caps have been retained is by verifying the presence or absence of the lenses on the sloughed skin from the head. Spectacle lenses resemble tiny contact lenses. If tape does not work, a drop of mineral oil applied to each eye once a week will keep them sufficiently hydrated until they come off with the next shed. Lip balm is another product that will help reduce the drying effects of retained eye caps.

Caution: If you're mistaken and attempt removal of the NEW spectacle lens, serious damage can result. When in doubt, do not attempt to remove retained lenses.

Dead skin that does not shed from the tail tip is also potentially serious. Each time retained dead skin gets damp and then dries out, it expands

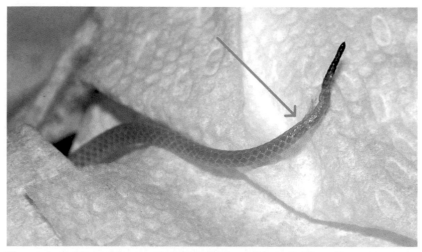

The retained skin on this corn resulted in the loss of the end of its tail.

and contracts. This has a constricting effect and can cut off blood flow to the tip of the tail. The usual result is necrosis (*dead tissue*) that will fall off during subsequent sheds. Essentially your snake's tail will become shorter. Unlike lizards that regeneratelost tails, any length of tail lost on a corn is gone forever. Inspect your corn each time it sheds to ensure that all the dead skin was removed. If you notice skin on the tail, do not try to pull it off dry. Apply mineral oil to this area with a cotton swab. Let it soak for several hours before attempting removal.

If treating your corn for sores or cuts, postpone the application of topical medications until after the shedding process. Likewise avoid using any pesticides or air fresheners around your snake during this time. When the skins are separating, the new skin is highly absorbent. Anything applied directly to the snake and even chemicals in the air are quickly absorbed. Overdoses are not uncommon and deaths have been attributed to toxic absorption during this extra-sensitive period.

Caution: Your snakes should be relocated if your home is being treated for insects or other pests. Any toxins used to eradicate pests will not be safe for serpents. Most pesticide companies advertise that their products are safe for use around household pets, but snakes have a higher propensity for absorbing pollutants than most mammals.

Chapter SIX: BREEDING

A mating pair of Reverse Okeetee corn snakes.

Breeding corns in captivity is relatively simple, but carries with it a great responsibility. If you're not prepared or not sure what you'll do with the babies, do not breed your corns. Feeding dozens of hungry baby snakes is not only expensive, but each one requires its own cage. Much time will be required to maintain their health. There are enough unwanted pets in the world today without selfishly contributing to a "disposable pet" mentality.

Just as important as keeping feeding and shedding records, documenting breeding events is recommended for future reference. Not only will this help you plan for subsequent breeding seasons, but your data could contribute to future collaborative research.

Determining Proper Gender

Of course, the first prerequisite to breeding is making sure you have a male and a female. Since the sexual organs of corns are not visually obvious like most mammals, determining their genders is sometimes difficult. No matter which method you use, when possible, it's always a good idea to get more than one opinion from experienced snake keepers. If your corns were not properly sexed, there is no serious consequence other than a disappointing lack of production. Combat between adult male corns is not common and I've never known injury to result.

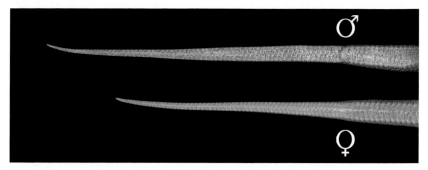

Note the long, gradual taper of the male tails compared to the abrupt and short taper of the female's.

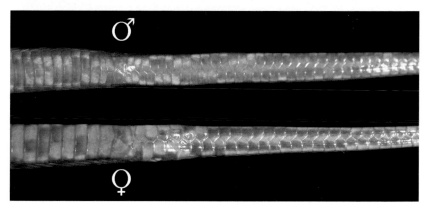

Sight Sexing is a successful method for the experienced snake keeper. Only after comparing hundreds of corns of different sizes is it possible to determine gender visually. Generally speaking, the tails of male corns are slightly longer, but don't rely on this distinction for positive identification. I've seen adult females with tails longer than those of most males. Regarding visual sexing, the most reliable anatomical difference between males and females is the shape of the tails rather than the length.

Unlike the female corns whose genitalia is not located in the tail, the male's hemipenes are actually in the tail, aft of the cloaca (*anal opening*). The tail base of the male tends to remain the same general width further than that of the female. Instead of measuring in inches, I'll use sub-caudal (*below cloaca*) scale counts to demonstrate general differences between sexes. The female's tail width tapers from the vent, back three to five sub-caudal scales. In males, the tail base is approximately the same width for 10-17 sub-caudals before tapering.

For neonates, there are several methods that are generally effective, but few of them are 100% accurate. Most are potentially damaging to the snake. The most commonly practiced method is that of **popping**. This technique requires skill and is not recommended unless you have been personally trained by an experienced snake keeper. If done incorrectly, your corn could be permanently damaged. Sterility is also possible from improper popping. Popping is usually only done on neonates, but not impossible for the seasoned snake keeper to successfully perform on adults.

Probing is a less practiced technique for hatchlings. Given the small and relatively delicate size of neonate corns, severe injury can result. Probes used for neonate corns are very small and it's easy to puncture vital organs and adjacent tissue. I have known people to accidentally stab a small probe completely through the side of a hatchling corn when the snake flinched in reaction to the procedure.

Safe and accurate probing of adults requires a very steady hand and the experience to know how much pressure is too much. This is another method of sexing that is better left to the experts. Complications from probing injuries can impair future breeding performance for males. Probing adults is less dangerous than for neonates, but still requires experience. Learning to probe snakes is not something that can be mastered from books. Just like popping, hands-on training is the only safe way to learn this delicate procedure.

Candling is a safe and non-invasive way to determine the sex of your corn. It is only effective on very young snakes and then only on albinos and other pale morphs. In a dimly lit room, place a small light against the tail base of the corn. On males, you will see two dark red lines running from the cloaca toward the tail tip. These represent the blood in the hemipenes. These lines usually extend seven to 14 sub-caudals from the vent. If you see any small, red lines in the female's tail, they will be from the vent, just three to five sub-caudals back. These represent the hemipenial homologs and are essentially functionless in females (Barker, pers. com.). Instead of using a small light, this procedure can be done by holding the neonate corn in the line of sight between you and any light in a dimly lit room.

Caution: The heat from the light can injure your snake so keep exposure to a minimum.

If all else fails, your adult corns will reveal their genders when introduced to other corns during the breeding season. Body language between snakes is virtually foolproof once you understand it. When any two adult snakes are introduced, they exhibit jerking and twitching body motions. It is a common myth that this indicates they are both males. If the jerking motions subside after a few minutes, this usually indicates they are a male and female that are sexually disinterested or they're both females. If both are males, the interactions intensify to what could be described as a shoving match. Both males will push each other around, often slamming their sparring partner against the sides of the cage. Biting may also occur. Rarely are corns hurt during these bouts, but the stress that is imposed on both males should be avoided. Separate them if this behavior is observed. If a mature male has been introduced to a female during the breeding season and she is not receptive to breeding, the chase is on. The female will repel advances and make every attempt to escape. This often results in the female wadded up in the confines of a small hide or in the water bowl. If the female is in some stage of egg development, she emits pheromones (*chemical attractants*) to which the male cannot resist. You will know in minutes if you have introduced a sexually mature male to a receptive female. More details will be discussed later in this chapter regarding sexual behavior.

The Breeding Season

In captivity, corns are typically bred between March and June in the United States. Brumation (*the serpent equivalent of hibernation*) is not imperative prior to breeding corns, but will increase your chances for success. 60-90 days is a typical brumation period. 75 days is common in the industry if temperatures are sufficiently low. Since it is easier to find cold places in your home during the winter months, this is the most convenient time to brumate in the United States. Snake breeders in the southern United States may find it necessary to manipulate temperatures artificially for a properly cold brumation. Here is a typical schedule for breeding corns in the United States.

Begin Pre-Brumation Fasting November 15th

You may begin earlier or later, but for demonstration purposes, I will use November 15th as the starting point for pre-breeding activi-

Note: The breeding details in this section are based on the illustrated timeline (right). The timing of your snakes' particular breeding events is dependant upon many nutritional and environmental factors that can alter breeding schedules so these dates constitute only an example of a breeding schedule.

Time line for
SMR # 467 female.
Breeding season 2005

November
— 15 Day Fast

December

— 75 Day Brumation

January

February

March — Bred — Shed

April — Shed — Lay

May

June — Shed — Lay

July

Nov. 15-30 fast
Dec. 1-Feb. 15 brumation
▓ heavy feeding
Mar. 10 post-brumation shed
Mar. 11-13 bred
Apr. 10 pre-lay shed
Apr. 18 lay
Apr. 28 post-lay shed
Jun. 9 pre-lay shed
Jun. 17 lay
Jun. 28 post-lay shed

ties. Corns should never be below 80° F (27° C) for more than a few days unless they are being brumated and only when they have empty stomachs. Prior to brumating, I recommend allowing 15 days after their last feeding for digestion and defecation. Per this example schedule, there should be no feeding November 15th through February 15th.

Caution: Do not brumate corns that are under weight or unhealthy. Brumation could further degrade their immune systems.

Begin Brumation December 1st

Maintain a temperature range of 45-65° F (7-18° C). The target temperature is in the low 50s F (11° C), but very brief periods down to mid 30s F (-1° C) are usually safe. Brumating between 65° F and 75° F (18-23° C) is acceptable, but in that temperature range, corns are burning calories at unsafe levels. If you are unable to maintain temperatures below 65° F (7-18° C), I recommend a shorter brumation period of 45 to 60 days. There can be periods of a few days above and below this temperature range without adversely affecting your animals. If you are unable to maintain temperatures below 70° F (21° C), do not attempt brumation.

Darkness is preferred, but if you cannot offer your corns a predominantly dark brumation, at least give them a good hide that allows the least amount of light penetration. Change the drinking water weekly. I recommend recording the high and low temperatures each day on a calendar for future reference.

Begin Warm-Up February 15th

Some say it's necessary to raise the snake's body temperature up to the 80s F (27° C) gradually, but there were many seasons I abruptly converted the brumating breeders from cold to warm in one day and had normal egg production.

Note: Exposure to temperatures over 90° F (32° C) is not only dangerous to corns, but can kill sperm in males. Avoid situations where adult males can lie directly on overheated surfaces.

Begin Heavy Feeding Schedule

Your corn should not have experienced significant weight loss during a properly cold brumation, but aggressive feeding is still recommended to prepare them for breeding. When not breeding, I recommend feeding adult female corns one appropriately sized meal item every five to seven days. During the breeding season, fat and carbohydrate levels in the females need to be high to facilitate egg production. If not in some stage of shedding, I feed the breedable females one meal item every four to five days. Males should be fed one appropriately sized meal item every seven to 10 days during the breeding season. Males require fewer calories since their nutritional needs are much lower than those of egg-producing females.

The first one or two stools after brumation may be runny and discolored. Atypical stools are not uncommon after brumation, but if the third post-brumation stool appears to be abnormal, consult a qualified reptile veterinarian immediately. Intestinal disorders and/or medications to correct them can adversely affect egg production so if required, starting those medication regimens as soon as possible may have the least negative impact on egg production.

Breeding Usually Begins By Mid March

Generally speaking, after brumation, each shed will signal a breeding event. The post-brumation shed usually occurs two to three weeks after warm-up. There are exceptions, but most breeders begin to introduce couples shortly before or after this shed.

Note: On rare occasions, females will not be receptive to males until after their second post-brumation shed.

It doesn't matter if the male is introduced to the female's cage or vice versa. Some corn snake breeders don't put pairs together until the female is visually swelling from egg development. This is more of a convenience than a necessity. Since the female can retain sperm from copulations prior to ovulation (*transfer of eggs from ovaries to oviduct*), you need not wait for visual evidence of egg development. As a rule, if the female is receptive and copulation occurs, viable eggs should be expected. I recommend that if you intend to breed males to more than one female, limit the number of copulations for each female. Male corns can copulate up to four times per day and that can severely deplete sperm stores. The result can be the potentiality that subsequent females will not receive enough sperm for desirable fertility rates. Since I use one male for several females each season, I restrict the number of copulations to three times per female. If the male is not slated to breed multiple females, I leave them together, separating them only periodically for feedings. If copulation is not witnessed, I recommend the introduction of the pairs at least once a week for several hours to increase your chances of getting viable eggs. If you have back-up males of acceptable genetic desirability, consider introducing a different male if the female is not initially receptive.

Note: For several days during their shedding process, males may not be interested in breeding.

Breeding Behavior and Procedures

Courtship and breeding among snakes is very different from that of most animals. It is therefore interesting to observe, but keep human interference to a minimum. Not only can injury occur as a result of distractions during copulation, but any interference now may prevent the successful conclusion of breeding.

If the female is sexually mature and receptive to the advances of a sexually mature male, copulation will often begin within minutes of introduction. The courtship begins with the usual introductory body language of flinching and jerking rhythmically and often synchronously. The male will attempt to position himself on top of the female. Sometimes, males will force themselves upon reluctant females so successful copulation will result. It is rare for corns, but like many other species, male corns will sometimes bite the neck or head of the female to force her co-operation. Keep an eye on such occurrences, but intervene only if the female's nostrils are blocked by the male's bite. This biting is extremely rare if the female is receptive. The male will move forward to gain a position where the tails of both snakes are parallel. This is often achieved by pushing his chin down on the female's back while systematically moving toward her head. The "chinning" stimulus from the male communicates his intentions, which usually results in her co-operation. Once the male senses their vents are parallel, he moves his tail over the side of the female, which encourages the raising of her tail. Sometimes the male will use the end of his tail to lift hers for easier access. When his vent touches hers, in the blink of an eye, he everts one hemipenis (*one of the paired hemipenes*) and inserts it into her cloaca. This happens so quickly, you will likely not realize they're joined until you notice his alignment tactics have ceased. They usually lie still for several minutes except for periodic spasms from the male. After a few minutes, the hemipenis is engorged with blood and is only partially exposed at

A pair of Okeetee corn snakes copulating. Photo by Ryan Moss.

the base of his vent. It appears as a dark red or purple muscle from his vent, going into hers. For the next 10-20 minutes, both tails will slowly and simultaneously wave back and forth and up and down. You will notice considerable swelling in the female where the engorged hemipenis is engaged. It is important not to disturb them at this time.

The copulation event is usually complete in 15-30 minutes, but longer or shorter than that is not uncommon. When deposition of sperm is complete, the male will slowly remove his hemipenis from the female. Upon retraction, there will be spillage of semen. It is usually yellow in color and very viscous. It is not uncommon for some blood to be in this semen spillage and is usually no cause for alarm. However, premature disengagement can sometimes cause injury to one or both snakes and occasionally cage litter can adhere to the male's exposed hemipenis, causing retraction complications. If you notice any foreign debris

Copulating corn snakes. Photo by Ryan Moss.

(usually substrate bedding) protruding from the vent of the male after retraction, slowly remove the object(s) or infection may result. I usually do not introduce that pair again for 24 hours if multiple copulations are scheduled. Multiple breedings are recommended to increase fertility, but one breeding usually yields an acceptable brood of fertile eggs.

Note: I recommend housing corns individually, but if you house pairs together, know that many copulations will occur in the course of a few weeks. This will essentially exhaust sperm stores in the male quickly.

Pre Egg-Laying Shed

Approximately 30-35 days after conception, the pre egg-laying shed should occur. 20 to 55 days after conception is not uncommon. Do not feed the female again until after she lays her eggs. Remove the water bowl and replace it with a small one she cannot fit into. This will reduce the chance of her laying eggs in water. Eggs that are laid in water rarely hatch.

Nest Box

This shed signals the best time to put a nest box in the cage. I recommend using damp sphagnum moss as a nest medium. Vermiculite (*a mica mineral product*) holds moisture but is very messy. It adheres to the snake and usually ends up stuck to every surface in the cage. Peat moss is not recommended as it can become packed into the mouth and nostrils of the female as she excavates a laying site. Vermiculite also lacks the "earthy" smell of natural substrates such as moss. The scent of sphagnum moss offers an instinctive attraction and virtually assures that she will lay the eggs where you want them. Use chlorine-free water to dampen the nest box substrate. No water should be standing in the bottom of the container. The minimum nest box for an adult corn measures 12" long x 8" wide x 5" tall. The lid should have a hole at one end that is twice the diameter of the adult female. She will investigate the inside of the container almost immediately. She may even stay in the moss for a few days, but will usually remain outside the nest box until a day or two before she lays her eggs. Inspect the moss daily to ensure it doesn't contain feces from the female. This could contaminate the eggs when they are laid. If you are not using a lid on the nest box, the moss will dry out so occasional spraying with water may be necessary. I do not recommend allowing the male or other females in the cage at this time. Females that are ready to lay eggs usually control the nest box in communal situations, but if they don't, it's possible that the eggs could be deposited outside the nest box. This could result in the death of the embryos.

The eggs are usually laid five to 14 days after this shed, with the average being 7-8 days. Do not rely on your snake doing this by the book though. I have had corns lay their eggs the day after shedding. Therefore, prepare a hatching container now so you are ready when the eggs are laid. Likewise, set up and test your incubator. If you're not using an incubator, have a location in your home prepared to incubate the eggs.

At this stage of development, you should be able to count the eggs in your corn by the corresponding bulges. The back half of your snake should be at least 50% fatter than usual and the skin should be stretched to the point of showing between the scales. It is rare, but sometimes this is not the pre-laying shed it appears to be. Just to be safe, introduce the male the day after this shed. If they do not copulate within 30 minutes, you can expect eggs to be laid in approximately a week. If they do breed, it's usually a sign that even though you think you're seeing eggs ready to be laid, they are actually full-sized, unfertilized ova (*eggs*). Usually infertile eggs will be passed very soon after this shedding event, but if you're lucky, the test breeding will result in fertilization and her next shed will be the signal that she will lay her eggs in about one week.

The digestive system of your corn is in direct competition with the reproductive system at this time. This means that all other organs in her body have been pushed aside (always forward) by the bulging oviducts. Therefore, little or no digestion should be occurring now. Dystocia (*a complication that impedes or prohibits the laying of eggs*) can result if fecal production or storage conflicts with oviposition (*egg laying*).

Preparing the Egg Container

Most breeders use plastic storage boxes for incubating corn snake eggs. Almost any clean plastic or glass container will suffice. The container should be at least 240 cubic inches (3,900 cu cm) with a minimum height of four inches (10 cm). This should safely accommodate one clutch of corn snake eggs. I do not recommend more than one clutch per container. This reduces the chances of getting babies from one clutch confused with others. Some breeders perforate the sides of the container with air holes for ventilation. If you do use air holes, I recommend that they be very small and few in numbers. I don't use any air holes in my incubation containers and find this fundamental to my hatching success. Sometimes, too much ventilation contributes to dehydration and the subsequent death of the embryos. To exchange air in the hatching container, open the box once each week for one or two minutes.

There are several different hatch mediums available at most garden supply stores. Sphagnum or peat moss, vermiculite, and perlite (*a mineral product of lava*) are the most commonly used incubating substrates. Peat and sphagnum moss are acidic and have some bactericidal properties, but since perlite and vermiculite are non-organic, I consider these the best substrates to use for incubation. I have used damp paper towels under eggs, but battled fungal growth throughout most of the incubation period.

Caution: When opening the bag of whichever substrate you have selected, if you no 'ce a chemical or petroleum smell, do not use it. Take it back to the store and consider buying your incubation substrate elsewhere. Eggs absorb whatever they're in contact with and even trace amounts of toxins can kill fragile embryos.

There is sometimes a fine line between initially making the incubation substrate too moist or too dry. When in doubt, opt for making it too dry. While dehydration is a deadly enemy to incubating eggs, it is easy to detect and quickly correctable. Overly wet substrate is equally dangerous. Often, the first sign that the substrate is too moist is the discoloration of eggs, indicating dead embryos. They essentially drown from the excessive moisture's interference with respiration by the embryos through the semi-permeable egg shells.

Snake breeders mix their incubation substrates in different ways using different materials, but here are some recipes that work well for me. When using sphagnum or peat moss, soak it in dechlorinated water for 10-30 minutes. Do not use water from water softening devices. The sodium or potassium levels are unsafe for developing embryos. Wring out the moss by squeezing it in your hands for several seconds or until the water stops draining. A 1.0" to 1.5" (2.5-3.8 cm) substrate depth is recommended. Whichever moss you use, a blanket of dampened sphagnum moss completely covering the eggs decreases the chances of dehydration. Close the lid of the container and place it in the incubator or designated incubation area for several hours to allow the substrate to absorb the moisture and for temperature stabilization. If you are mixing the substrate less than one hour before setting up the eggs, be sure to use water that is the same temperature as the cage where the eggs were laid. Sudden temperature changes can sometimes cause the death of corn snake embryos.

I use a combination of coarse vermiculite and perlite as an incubation substrate. Fine grade vermiculite can be used in conjunction with perlite, but I don't recommend using fine vermiculite alone. It's not coarse enough to allow air flow beneath the eggs. Coarse vermiculite alone has served snake breeders well for many years, but I like to add the perlite for increased substrate ventilation since pieces of perlite are two to three times larger than coarse vermiculite. For increased ventilation, mix two parts of perlite with three parts of coarse vermiculite. Mix 4.5 to five parts of dry substrate with one part of pure water (not tap water). One formula for mixing dry substrate with water c for equal parts by weight. I find this dangerously confusing if s one mixes the two ingredients by volume instead of weight. I a d essentially result in vermiculite soup and the embryos woul n almost immediately. It takes many hours for the substrate lly absorb the water. Don't be hasty and add water too soon because you thought it was excessively dry. It's much better to use an incubating substrate that is slightly dry than one that is too damp. After mixing, put a 1.0" to 1.5" (2.5-3.8 cm) damp substrate depth in the hatching container.

There are a couple of popular methods for testing the substrate's moisture content. After 24 hours of mixing it with water, grab a handful of the damp substrate. Squeeze it in your fist using approximately ½ of your strength. If water runs out of the substrate, it's too wet. While holding your fist with your thumb pointing up, slowly release your grip. If it crumbles out of your hand, it's too dry. If it remains in a pack the shape of your grip, it has the proper amount of moisture. Another simple test to evaluate the moisture level of the hatching medium after mixing is to wait 48 hours after closing the container of dampened substrate. There should be condensation somewhere on one or more of the inside surfaces of the container. If there is an area of condensation only a few inches in diameter on one or more of the walls or on the ceiling of the container, there is adequate moisture in your substrate. If more than half the sides and/or top are dripping with water, it's far too moist. Remove half of the dampened substrate and replace it with dry substrate. That should correct the problem and in 48 hours, condensation areas should form again. I then fill a one inch diameter (2.5 cm) receptacle with water and place it in the corner of the incubation container. This facilitates ambient humidity within the container without subjecting the eggs to direct watering. The lid from a soda bottle is perfect for the job and takes up little space.

Caution: Never spray water directly on the eggs. If you add water to the incubation substrate, do so by pouring or spraying the water on the inside walls of the container so it will leach through the substrate over a period of a few hours.

If you are using an incubator, 80-85° F (27-29° C) is a safe incubation temperate range. There are many models of incubators commercially available to the snake breeder, but you don't need to be an engineer or

A typical clutch of corn snake eggs.

carpenter to build one that will do a professional job of hatching corn snake eggs. Check web sites for instructions on how to build your own.

For years, I hatched all my snakes without incubators. Living in the Midwestern United States as I did and given that the eggs were laid during the summer months, there were places in my home that were ideal for incubation. Most closets and cabinets do not have air conditioning vents and if kept closed, often maintain ideal corn snake incubating temperatures in the central and southern United States.

Egg Laying

You should be checking the nest box daily since the female's last shed. The last day or two before she lays the eggs, she will likely spend most of her time in the nest box. She will push the substrate to one end of the nest box so she can lay the eggs on a clean, bare surface. As the eggs are laid, they are covered with a sticky substance that acts as a bonding agent. This sticky substance essentially glues the eggs to whatever they're in contact with at the time they're laid. Occasionally, corns will lay their eggs without this substance and the eggs will not stick together. It's not clear why this happens, but it surely is the result of a deficiency. Most corns position the eggs one after another to build the egg clump into a structure. The advantages of such formations are obvious.

1. If not bonded together in one mass, just jarring a log in the forest that contains a clutch of corn snake eggs could result in the toppling and disorientation of some or all of the eggs. Since the embryo is positioned above the yolk of the egg near an air pocket, changing the egg's orientation would essentially guarantee its death.

2. Predation from serpents would be easy if the eggs were not clumped together. There are many egg eating snakes that would find it impossible to swallow an entire "mound" of corn snake eggs but easy to devour the entire clutch, one egg at a time if not connected.

3. Probably the most valuable benefit from the eggs being stuck together is their united ability to share resources. Since the ground is moist and the egg shells are semi-permeable, if the outside eggs experience dehydration from increased exposure, the moisture absorbed from the ground by the bottom eggs is transferred to them by way of osmosis. Likewise, heat or the expulsion of heat is transferred when sudden temperature changes occur. The connectivity of all the eggs by semi-permeable shells communally uniting them is one reason they hatch at approximately the same time. I have noticed that eggs not attached to the clutch can sometimes hatch days before or after the united ones.

The female should be allowed to lay the eggs in privacy. There is little you can do to help her unless you discover that she is having trouble laying one or more of the eggs. Check periodically, but don't be a nuisance. If you notice she is unable to pass an egg, (*a condition called dystocia*), consult a snake breeder or qualified reptile veterinarian immediately. It will be obvious if any are retained. The egg laying process usually takes from one to 24 hours. Count the eggs, and if more than one hour has passed since the last one was laid, consider seeking help from a breeder or veterinarian.

Corns generally lay 10-20 eggs per clutch. Of course, fewer or more than that are not uncommon. The amount and size of the eggs are influenced by genetics, environment, nutrition, and fertility.

A Caramel Motley corn snake laying eggs. Animal courtesy of John Cherry.

Wait until all the eggs have been laid before harvesting them. This gives them time to become bonded together and affords the female the privacy she deserves to get the job done. The drying process for the adhesive substance takes only 20-30 minutes, after which time the egg surfaces will feel leathery. You may collect the eggs after the last one is dry.

Incubation

It is very common for some of the eggs to be infertile. Especially the last one(s) laid. If any of the eggs appear to be infertile, remove them from the group. Bad eggs are usually very easy to disconnect since they seldom have the adhesive coating that the viable ones do. Infertile eggs are usually a yellowish color and lack the white, leathery shell of the fertile ones. Since infertile eggs sometimes look viable, one way to distinguish the bad ones from the good ones is to candle them. In a dimly lit or dark room, put a small flashlight against the egg. If it's viable, you'll see many red blood veins. If it's infertile, none will be visible. Don't let the light heat up the egg. This can happen in seconds so keep contact with the light to a minimum. If you don't have a small light, cut a ¼" hole in the center of a piece of paper. Lay this over the flashlight beam and set the egg on the lighted hole you cut in the paper.

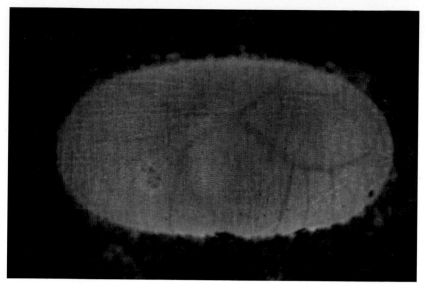
Note the veins in this seven day old fertile corn snake egg. Photo by Ryan Moss.

Some fertile eggs will not exhibit veins until they are several days old so if you don't see evidence of veins, check again a few days later.

If any of the fertile eggs are not stuck to others, make a small dot on the top center of each egg with a pencil in case they are jarred out of original position. Do not use an ink pen or marker as the ink can poison the embryo. For the first 48 hours, the eggs can be repositioned if necessary, but after that time, their orientation should not be changed or the embryo inside could die.

Unlike mammals that exchange vital nutrients by way of umbilical attachment to their mothers, once the eggs are laid, corns must respire through their shells in order to survive and develop. Microscopic pores in the egg shell allow the transfer of water and gases to and from the embryo. They respire by drawing in oxygen and expelling CO_2 through the porous shell. Therefore, the substrate under the eggs and any covering over them must facilitate the exchange of these gases. Since moss and paper are also permeable, if used to cover the eggs, they should not interfere with this process.

I prefer to emulate nature whenever possible. Dirt, moss and leaf litter are likely the only coverings on wild corn snake eggs so sphagnum

Lift the damp moss weekly to inspect the eggs.

moss is the natural choice for covering incubating eggs.

Place the eggs on the incubation substrate. Very gently push the eggs down into the substrate until the bottom row is half planted. Regardless of the substrate you chose as an incubation medium, I recommend covering all the eggs with damp sphagnum moss. Some breeders use a single sheet of newspaper, but I believe the moss allows more air circulation around the eggs. Covering the eggs is not necessary if no ventilation holes are in your incubation container, but a damp sphagnum moss covering will minimize the chances of dehydration.

Note: The eggs can be completely buried in the substrate provided it is coarse enough to provide ample ventilation. I prefer not to do this so I can monitor the health and progress of the eggs during the incubation process.

If you use damp sphagnum moss, lift it once a week to inspect the eggs. If using a water cup inside the incubation container to increase ambient humidity, check and refill it if necessary. If any molds or fungi are in the moss, rinse and wring it out or completely replace it. If any of the eggs are covered with fungus or mold, this is often a sign that the embryo is dead or dying. I have had limited success with brushing off the growth by using a stiff brush, but it's more common that those eggs

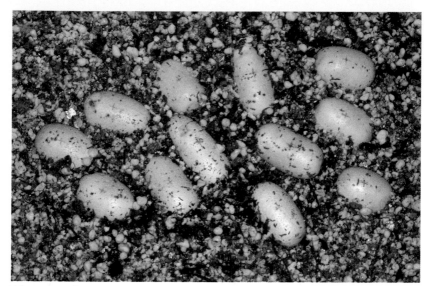

Disconnected eggs should be marked with a pencil in case they are moved from their original orientation. Brown spots on the eggs are harmless stains from the sphagnum moss covering.

cannot be saved. Do not spray water directly on the eggs and I recommend that you not let water get on them at all. This can clog the pores in the surface of the egg shell. Likewise, brushing off any growth on the surface can contribute to clogging of the pores by forcing micro particles into them. Usually such organic growths on the eggs in the last days of development can be removed without harming the embryo.

Before placing the egg box into the incubator or designated incubation area you have chosen, mark it with applicable identification associated with the parents and the date the eggs were laid. You cannot collect too much data on snake keeping events. I find photographic documentation to be invaluable in this digital era. Never pass up a photo opportunity. Not only do pictures reinforce your data, but you never know when you'll be fortunate enough to get that "one in a million" corn snake photograph.

The ideal temperature range for hatching corns is 80-85° F (27-29° C). Within this range, the corns should hatch in 60 days, plus or minus three days. Above that temperate range, but below 90° F (32° C), they can hatch in as few as 50 days, but some of these embryos will die from excessive temperatures. At lower temperatures, they will take longer

to hatch and if too far below that range, deformities
and even death can result.
In the late 1970s, Gary
Evans of Wichita, Kansas,
incubated a clutch of corns
at approximately 70° F (21°
C). When the eggs had not
hatched after day 92 of incubation, we cut them
open. Some of the snakes
inside were alive, but almost
completely fused together.
After removing the shells

The ideal temperature range for hatching corns is 80-85° F (27-29° C).

from some of them, their profiles were exactly that of the eggs they
were in. Other abnormalities from incubation deficiencies include deformed spines, depigmentation, complete pattern aberrancies (full stripes
are common), enlarged craniums, and other anatomical deformities.

At any time during incubation, if you discover dead eggs, remove them
as carefully as possible without causing excessive pressure or movement to the others. Do not tilt or otherwise alter the orientation of the
healthy eggs. It may be necessary to cut away bad eggs that are not
easily removed manually. Dead eggs not only attract fungal growth,
but can attract ants or flies. Phorid flies, members of the insect family
Phoridae (sometimes called carrion flies) are a particularly dangerous
threat to corn snake eggs. These insects are rarely attracted to living
eggs, but their maggots literally feast on dead ones. In the process, the
maggots will invade adjacent living eggs and in sufficient populations,
can cause those to die. The absence of air holes in the incubating
container helps reduce the threat of these flying pests.

In the first few weeks of incubation, there will be noticeable growth of
the eggs. This is mostly due to water absorption. I have had excessively moist substrates cause eggs to almost double in size. Despite
the exaggerated size of the egg, the corns that hatched from those
eggs were average in size.

Most corn snake eggs laid in the wild are in almost complete darkness
during the entire incubation period. I have hatched eggs in clear containers in rooms that were indirectly lit by window and overhead light-

ing most of the day. While hatch rates were acceptable, I have had better hatching success incubating in darkened rooms. Even in well lit rooms, if you're covering the eggs with damp sphagnum moss, sufficient darkness will be achieved.

Since corns take approximately 60 days to incubate at nominal temperatures, you should be inspecting them daily, starting about 55 days after they were laid. In the last week of incubation, the texture of the shells begins to change. They get softer and instead of the bright white look they've had throughout most of the incubation period, they slowly get darker. This is partially due to the egg shells getting thinner from the embryos robbing them of calcium in the final stages of development. Of course, by now, the size of the embryo dictates that it is almost fully in contact with the inside walls of the egg. It is even possible in some eggs to actually distinguish the pattern of the occupant. In the last few days before hatching, the eggs may become slightly puckered. It will remind you of dehydration, but this is normal. Not all eggs will pucker like this, but it is no cause for alarm if they do. Movement of the embryo inside is usually evident in the last few days before emergence.

Hatching

This is what all the hard work (and fun) has been about. It's hatching time. As much as you want to take in every moment of this event, don't overdo it. You will be the first thing the snakes see when they pip (*cut their egg shells*) and they are instinctively frightened of very large, moving objects in close proximity to them. Too much commotion near the eggs at this time can delay hatching or even worse, cause premature emergence.

Since the shell of a corn snake egg is not brittle, it takes something sharp to cut it. The hatchlings are equipped with what we call an egg tooth positioned on the tip of their snouts. As they attempt to push out of the egg to get much needed oxygen for their developing lungs, they co-incidentally make cuts in the shell. Most of the time, many slits are made, predominantly at the top of the egg. If a sibling is situated directly above their egg, they will sometimes need to cut the sides to prepare an exit. For the next 24 hours, their heads are sticking out of the cuts they made but they should not emerge until their yolk is fully absorbed.

Corn snakes absorb their yolks before emerging from their eggs.

Within 48 hours of the first pip, all the snakes should have sliced through their shells. Sometimes eggs not connected to the main clutch will pip later than 48 hours after the first ones. If all eggs are not pipped within 48 hours of the first one, consult an experienced breeder for recommendations. There is not enough oxygen in the eggs at this stage of development to prevent suffocation.

Usually about 24 hours after pipping, the corns will emerge. If a corn stays in the egg 48 hours or more after pipping, something's usually wrong. Since it's getting oxygen by virtue of having its head out, there is usually no need to get invasive until you discover the source of the problem. Sometimes it's because they are deformed and incapable of maneuvering out of the egg, but sometimes the snake has wrapped its yolk stem around itself and is incapable of absorbing the yolk. It's fairly complicated to successfully free the snake and have it survive, but it can be done. If completely extracting it from the egg (yolk and all) and immediately putting it in very wet cotton balls or paper towels does not facilitate yolk absorption, your last recourse is to sever the yolk stem. This is rare and you will hopefully never see it, but advice from experienced breeders regarding the complete procedure is advised. Most veterinarians are not experienced enough to deal with natal reptile emergencies like this, but most snake breeders deal with it annually.

Multiple cuts from a corn snake's egg tooth.

If you get too nosey, some corns will duck back into their eggs. This is home for them so they're comfortable inside. The difference now is that they are respiring by lung instead of through their egg shell. They will come back out, but don't tempt fate by annoying them too much. If you persist, some corns may prematurely exit their eggs. This is potentially deadly. If they emerge before completely absorbing their yolk, they have been robbed of vitally important nutrition. I give a snake in this situation a 50/50 chance for survival. If they leave the egg only having partially absorbed the yolk, you must immediately put them in a very damp environment. I recommend having a container with hatching temperature water standing by when corns are hatching. Place the snake into 1/8" to 1/4" of water and immediately cover the container to achieve total darkness. Keep the container warm. Note how much of the yolk stem is unabsorbed so you can evaluate progress. Check on the snake every hour to determine if it is absorbing. Since this protruding yolk stem is a direct line into the stomach of the snake, it is allowing germs to get into the snake's system. Germs that were not in the egg and were never meant to enter the snake. The water must remain clean so change it every few hours. If after several hours, no absorption progress is made, cut the yolk stem, leaving ½" protruding. Place the snake back in clean water. If it has not absorbed the stem within six hours, move the snake to a container of dry aspen bedding. This will essentially dehydrate the stem and not unlike the umbilicus of mammals, it will dry up and fall off. Without this nutrient rich first meal, the corn may not survive, but a 50/50 chance is better than none at all. If snakes with this rough start do survive, they usually grow slowly and sometimes never reach full size.

Remove the vacant egg shells as quickly as possible. The fluids still inside them attract insects. In a 48 hour snake hatching period, Phorid flies have time to start a complete generation of future flying pests inside these nutrient-rich egg shells.

Emergence

Depending on genetics and pre-natal conditions, hatchling corn snakes are usually 6-16 inches (15-40 cm) long. The average is over eight inches (20 cm). Most of the corn snakes will hatch within 24 hours. Don't worry about the oldest ones slithering over pipped eggs that are still occupied. This has been going on for millions of years. Many newly hatched snakes often stay together until their first shed. In corns, that's approximately seven days after they hatch. The moist environment that was essential for successful incubation is exactly what they need to keep their skins moist during their first ecdysis (*shed*). In the wild, after the first shed, the litter disburses and they venture out in search of their first live meal. Communal housing is safe until their first shed is complete. They cluster together, vying for the moist (and dark) core of the snake pile. Damp sphagnum moss will help ensure that their first shed is a normal one.

It is now time to set up your young corns in their own cages. Follow the housing, heating, and feeding recommendations outlined earlier in the book and you will enjoy producing corns for years to come.

Chapter SIX: GENETICS

Candy Cane corn snakes are very popular in the hobby.

Herpetoculture (*the keeping and breeding of reptiles or amphibians*) has come a long way in the past 40 years and corns have been front-runners in the booming reptile industry. Sometimes referred to as the guppies of the snake world, corns have the greatest color and pattern diversity of any captive-bred reptile. This is largely due to the ease with which corns are bred in captivity.

As recently as 30 years ago, it was rare to see corns distinctly different from the so-called "normal" ones. The pale looking keys corn (aka rosy rat), the South Dade County, Florida (aka Miami phase) corn, the Jasper County, South Carolina (aka Okeetee) corn and the many different color shades of the nominate races dominated the hobby. Dr. H. Bernard Bechtel is credited with introducing the albino (*amelanistic*) corn snake to herpetoculture. Once Dr. Bechtel proved the albino gene in corns to be recessive in heritable nature and therefore had predictable breeding outcome, the hunt was on for the next recessive trait. Since then, there have been only a handful of recessive traits discovered in corns, but the exponential combinations of the different colors and patterns appear to be endless. Each year, one or more new "looks" of corns are revealed, building upon the relatively few recessive and co-dominant traits available to date. Every few years, a new gene is discovered, adding yet another branch to the sprawling family tree of corn snakes.

Genetics is merely the language with which we explain the mechanics of heritable traits. At first glance, the science of genetics seems complicated, but like anything we desire to learn, once you become familiar with the language of corn snake genetics, you will thoroughly enjoy performing equations to predict the progeny of corn snake pairings.

Most of the popular corn snake morphs today are examples of simple recessive traits. Recessive traits are ones that will not be promoted unless both partners in the pairing are carrying that trait. They can be homozygous (*displaying the look of the gene*) or heterozygous (*possessing the gene without showing the trait*). One example is the amelanistic corn. If you breed an amelanistic corn to a corn that is neither homozygous nor heterozygous for the amelanistic gene, all the offspring will be normally colored and heterozygous for amelanism.

The science of Mendelian genetics is named after its founder, Gregor Mendel (1822-1884). The fundamentals of his early genetic observations have changed very little in almost 1,200 years.

At the time of this writing, there are at least ten simple recessive color and pattern traits popularly recognized in corns. By combining those traits with each other and with many of the non-recessive ones, there are well over 100 different looking corn lines that have been named and are currently being marketed. In addition to combining the simple recessive color and pattern morphs of corns to achieve complex combinations, we now have co-dominant traits. To date, there are only two co-dominant corn snake traits. The first and oldest co-dominant trait recognized in corns is the motley/striped gene. The relationship between motley and striped corns does not fit neatly into our perception of a co-dominant trait, but if you breed a striped corn to a motley corn, normal (*wild type*) corns will not be produced. In my experience of breeding striped corns to motley corns, I have never produced purely striped corns. My results have always been motlies and striped motlies. Therefore, the relationship of those morphs is not what I would term traditional co-dominance since motley seems to dominate the striped trait in such pairings.

One of the latest and most exciting discoveries in the family of corn snakes is the ultra gene/trait. This one is undeniably co-dominant, but only with amelanism. Therefore, it will not behave co-dominantly when bred to non amelanistic corns. Because ultras are so new to herpetoculture, we don't yet how much they can vary in appearance. This is one of the few corn snake traits in which not all of its members can be readily identified visually. Ultra/ultramel corns are not hypomelanistic corns. Ultra corns look so much like hypomelanistic (hypo) corns, the only way to distinguish between them is through breeding trials. As a rule, neonate ultramels generally appear to have half the melanin (black color pigment) of "normal" corns. This gives the pupil of the eye the appearance of being dark red. The normally black scales of the ultras and ultramels are usually light black or gray, just like most hypos. The dark red pupils of neonates change to black at maturity.

Many thanks to Charles Pritzel and Connie Hurley for making a proper determination of the genetic mechanics of this morph. Without their expertise in the field of genetics, it might have taken many more years to determine the inheritance of the ultra gene/trait.

The breeding results for corns with one simple recessive trait is fairly straight-forward, but when other recessive or co-dominant genes are added to the mix, predicting the results is more complicated and potentially confusing. Virtual programs are available on the Internet to assist you in predicting the outcome of your corn snake breeding projects. The most popular (and the most comprehensive in my opinion) was written by Noel (Mick) Spencer. We are very grateful that Mick offers his program free of charge. It can be downloaded by going to **http://www.mywebpages.comcast.net/spencer62/cornprog.html**. Query "Mick's progeny predictor" on your web browser if that URL does not direct you to the download page. Another informative web site that offers detailed information, tutorials, and instructions for predicting corn snake genetic outcomes is **http://www.serpwidgets.com/ genetics.html**, designed and owned by Charles Pritzel (aka Serpwidgets). Chuck also produces an annual publication called the Cornsnake Morph Guide. For more information about this invaluable guide, go to **http://www.cornguide.com**. Yet another comprehensive genetics calculator can be accessed on the web site of Daniel Bohle of Berlin and Michael Glaß of Klingenthal, both in Germany. You can access this informative tool by going to the Internet URL **http://www.kornnatterlexikon.de/calculator.** You don't need to read German to use this great corn snake genetics predictor. Connie Hurley, DVM, a veterinarian in the Chicago, Illinois area, offers a monthly newsletter *THERE'S JUST SOMETHING ABOUT CORNS* for a relatively token subscription price. Her publications are timed to coincide with the *seasons* of corns and Connie prides herself in offering the latest accurate data and tips pertinent to the corn snake hobby. A great deal of corn snake genetics information is presented in her articles. To subscribe to this monthly publication, go to **http://cccorns.com/Newsletter/newsletter.htm.**

Chapter SEVEN: ESCAPES

I never thought I would be dedicating a chapter to this subject, but I get so many phone calls and emails annually, I am compelled to share some helpful tips. I think a decent living could be made in a large city by offering a snake recovery service for run away snakes. There are some members of the household that just aren't going to sleep well until the family pet corn is safely returned to its cage.

Neonate corns are small and it is easy to imagine how difficult it could be to find one that is loose in your home, but adult corns are also very adept at hiding. I have learned a lot of tricks over the years of having so many corns, but friends, associates, and customers have taught me a few as well. While there are hundreds of effective ways to find corns that are cleverly eluding their owners, I will detail some of the most effective ones.

Corn snakes are territorial so once they call a place home (i.e. their cage), they are not comfortable anywhere else. This doesn't keep them from continually trying to escape though. Even when we offer them the best cuisine and accommodations, they still want to roam. Once corn snakes escape, most of them search for a way to get back

Tape traps are very effective in capturing escaped corn snakes.

into their cages. Unfortunately, in the process, they sometimes find better accommodations or fall victim to one of a hundred dangerous hazards in the average household. The cat, the furnace, the refrigerator compressor, the trash, the toilet, or just being in the wrong place at the wrong time. I have seen and heard it all from corns ending up in the spin cycle of the laundry to short circuiting computers. One of the most common myths is that they want to be in your bed. This is the one place I have never found a loose corn and I personally have never heard of someone finding one in bed with them. So Mom, no need to pull the comforter up that's draped over the edges of the bed. The one thing wayward corns are not looking for is human companionship.

Except for suggesting the old fashioned method of turning the house upside-down, the best advice for achieving a successful resolution to this emergency is to act quickly. The first 48 hours offer your best chance for finding it. First of all, corns are largely nocturnal so they cruise around at night in search of comfortable temperatures. As a rule, if they don't find what they seek, they hole up and try again the next night. After a couple of nights of not finding their cage, they finally strike out for parts unknown. For the first 48 hours, they are usually in the room from which they escaped or very close to it.

The most successful retrieval method is a tape trap. Akin to the fly paper concept, the idea is to leave a piece of tape where they will get stuck to it. Do not use excessively sticky tape or you will never get them off in one piece. Masking or painter's tapes are the best choices as they are not as sticky as most tapes, but sticky enough to entangle a corn. Of course, it would take a very large piece to tape up an adult corn, but neonates are incapable of escaping the grip of even small pieces of tape.

For neonate corns, a length of tape approximately 12" x 1/2" (30 x 1.3 cm) will suffice. When corns are loose, they tend to follow the walls in your home, so put the tape on the floor next to the wall. A piece next to each wall in the room where the escape happened is recommended. One or two pieces in adjoining rooms and hallways too. You can either curl both ends of the tape so it will stick to the floor with most of the sticky surface facing up or you can just let a piece fall to the floor like you would drop a piece of ribbon. Dropping it results in the tape landing on the floor in a random heap with sticky surfaces facing in more than one direction. I have found both ways to be equally effective. Roughly 75% of the snake owners that ask me for advice, report that they found their snakes with tape traps in the first 48 hours. Half of those found them the first night they set the traps. When removing the tape, sometimes warm water helps loosen the adhesive of the tape.

Caution: Never use glue boards sold for catching mice and insects. Your snake would never survive the removal process.

Some people set the snake's cage on the floor on its side. Placing it next to the wall forces the snake to detour around it. They often end up in the cage where they can be recovered the next morning. If they lived in their cage long enough to call it home, being territorial, they are instinctively attracted to it. If you can leave the heat source on, you enhance your chances for success since it's ordinarily so cool on the floor.

Funnel traps are another effective trap system although most people do not want to go to the trouble of making one. It requires cutting the nozzle end off a two liter or three liter plastic soda bottle. Reverse the funnel you removed and put it back on the bottle so the opening is now inside. Tape or staples work well to rejoin the severed end to the body of the bottle. Some use two bottles and join them for twice the length with entrances on both ends. This funnel trap will not attract them and the cylindrical shape of the bottle means the opening is not on the floor so you will need to lure them with bait. Common attractants to put inside the bottle include, bedding from its cage, a dead mouse, or bedding from a mouse cage. Not unlike the highly successful funnel traps for fish, once the snake is inside, it usually cannot find the exit

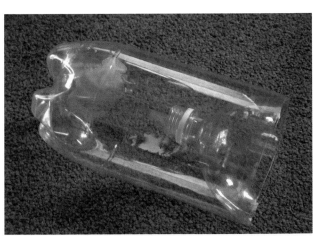

"Funnel" traps can be fashioned from plastic soda bottles.

opening. It just keeps nosing at the lowest part of the bottle until it gets tired and goes to sleep.

If you are not having success with traps, sometimes it's useful just to know where the snake is. Provided your corn is still in the house, there are several ways to discover its location. One is to sprinkle flour or salt on the floor next to the wall. This will not catch the snake, but as long as the dogs and cats in the house don't play in it, you will find snake tracks in the flour or salt. Then, you can concentrate your search in that area of the house. Since closets are a common place for them to hole up (especially inside shoes or pockets of clothing), putting salt or flour on the floor on both sides of closet doors can be effective. Escaped corns also seek out heat so the backs of refrigerators and freezers are ideal haunts since the area around the compressor is so warm. If the snake is large enough, place empty soda cans upright on the floor almost next to the wall. For example, if the snake has a girth of one inch, put the empty can ½" away from the wall. As it crawls along the wall at night, it might move the can. If you stack two cans, sometimes the cans will topple and awaken someone in the house. Just hope your best mouse-eating cat doesn't hear it first.

After 48 hours, the chance of finding your corn alive is greatly reduced. Keep the floors throughout the house uncluttered. Take up throw rugs and be careful not to step on the loose edges of carpets. Most snakes relish the feeling of hides that are snug against their backs. One customer told me he intentionally threw his dirty clothing all over the floor of his bedroom and the next day he shook the escapee out from one of his shirts. Several customers reported to me that they laundered their snakes that were hiding in piles of clothing ready for washing. Of course, the wash cycle killed those snakes quickly. Therefore, shake out clothing before tossing them into the washing machine. Cover floor and wall vents with fine mesh screen. Cover the vents of window air conditioners and keep lids on trash receptacles. Eliminate gaps at the bottom of your entry doors that are large enough for the snake to escape. Tape a temporary cardboard door sweep to the bottom of the door until you are able to secure it properly. Think "floor" because gaps and crevices at ground level are the most likely exits for wandering corns.

Of course, being proactive is always better than being reactive. Make sure everyone that handles your corn knows how important it is to keep the lid of the cage secure at all times. Have a house rule that children are not permitted to return the family corn to its cage without having another family member verify a secure closure. A lock on the cage might even be necessary when habitual violators or small children are involved. I have heard reports of corns crawling through their water bowl to get just sticky enough to literally slither up the glass sides of a tall cage.

Keep a small bowl of fresh water on the floor next to a wall in each room. Many corns are found dead from dehydration that might otherwise have been found alive if only water was available. Also, many escaped corns have been found fatally stuck to loose tape on storage boxes.

Chapter EIGHT: DISEASES
AND DISORDERS

Incomplete sheds can adversely affect the health of your corn.

Fortunately, diseases are rare in corns and most parasites are avoidable and easily eradicated. Since most corns in the hobby are captive-bred, the chance of acquiring one with parasites is rare. The best practice for detecting and treating potential problems and for reducing the possibility of contamination to your other pets is to quarantine any newly acquired snakes. Besides keeping newly acquired corns in separate cages, when possible, I recommend maintaining them in a different room for at least 60 days. Thoroughly wash your hands and forearms before and after handling any pets and make quarantined snakes the last pets you handle each day. This reduces the chances of cross contamination of diseases and parasites to and from your other pets.

The most common health problems in captive corns are environmentally stimulated. Since temperature is so critical in maintaining a corn's health, many problems are not disease initiated, but the result of improper housing. Therefore, it is essential that you first rule out any caging deficiencies before considering the possibility that your snake has a disease or parasites. Lack of adequate heat is the leading cause of poor health in captive corns. Refer to the **HOUSING** chapter for details.

Digestive Disorders

If cage conditions are proper and your corn exhibits an inability to properly digest food, it is likely infected with one or more of a host of organisms that can interfere with digestion. Poisoning is possible, but rare in corns. Be sure your corn is not exposed to any potentially toxic chemicals before attempting to diagnose digestive disorders.

Most corns perpetually harbor alien organisms without harm. These organic pests are kept in check by the snake's immune system and consequently do not adversely affect healthy corns. Some bacteria within the stomachs of corns are even essential for proper digestion. Others do not benefit them and if allowed to overpopulate, can cause severe problems and even death. In cases of immunodeficiency or sometimes in very young or very old corns, these uninvited free-loaders can be overwhelming. Common symptoms related to infestations of parasites or other disruptive organisms include:

* Runny, discolored or foul smelling stools
* Abnormal lack of appetite
* Regurgitation
* Stomach bloating
* Abnormally prolonged digestion

If your corn exhibits any of these symptoms, you should consult a qualified reptile veterinarian. Anytime your snake displays an abrupt or chronic change that is not the result of cage conditions or routine cycles like reproduction, shedding or brumation, medications may be required. Regurgitation is always serious and should never be accepted as normal. Your veterinarian may require a fresh sample of feces or a regurgitated meal so be prepared to act promptly. Do not freeze the sample. Refrigerate it in a previously unused plastic container and seal it to avoid contamination. Your vet will microscopically inspect the specimen to determine what medications will be most effective in treating your snake.

Regurgitation Syndrome

Since regurgitation is not unique to any one stimulus, we put it in the category of syndrome (*a group of symptoms that collectively apply to a disorder*). Anytime your corn regurgitates, you should be concerned. There are many reasons for a snake to regurgitate, but if you do not initiate post-regurgitation therapy following such an incident, your snake could die. Before outlining the common reasons for regurgitation in corn snakes, here is some very important advice about what to do immediately following such an event.

Post-Regurgitation Therapy

Corns expel most of their stomach acids when they regurgitate a meal. Since they have approximately 1/5 the metabolism of a mammal, it takes much longer to replenish those acids. If they are fed too soon after a regurgitation event, they will often regurgitate again. Successive regurgitations can be devastating. Unless the conditions that caused the first regurgitation are identified and corrected, recurring regurgitations are likely.

If you have corrected the cause of the regurgitation, wait seven to ten days before offering another meal, provided the snake is not in some stage of shedding. If it is, do not offer a meal until after that shed is complete. The next meal offering must be 25-75% smaller than usual. With reduced stomach acid stores, anything larger cannot be digested. For hatchling corns that are still eating one pinky mouse, I recommend feeding the head of a pinky once a week for three weeks. After that cycle, feed one cut-in-half pinky or the equivalent every seven days for the next three feedings. By this time, if all meals were digested completely, you may return to your normal feeding regimen. If any of these offerings are regurgitated, consult a qualified reptile veterinarian for evaluation. Ordinarily, after three successive regurgitations, most young corns will not survive without medication.

Common reasons for regurgitations in corns include:

* Temperature extremes or inadequate thermo-regulation
* Oversized meal
* Over handling

---

* Eating near or during a shedding event
* Nervousness
* Parasites or diseases
* Exposure to toxins

One of the most common reasons for regurgitation in corns is improper temperatures. Too hot, too cold, and even inadequate temperate zones within the cage from which to thermo-regulate have been known to cause regurgitation. Sometimes, just one night or a few hours of excessive or inferior temperatures is enough to cause a meal to be regurgitated. Like most snakes, corns move from one thermal zone to another to facilitate the timely digestion of meals. Remember that a corn snake's natural instinct to hide is almost always stronger than its desire to achieve proper body temperatures. Each thermal zone within the cage should have a hide so the snake is encouraged to utilize different zones in privacy. Corns are nocturnal and secretive. Staying hidden is their primary defense against predation. In cases of improper temperatures, the snake cannot digest a meal faster than it will decompose in the stomach. Flourishing bacteria within the meal item causes excessive swelling. When the swollen meal exceeds the capacity of the snake's stomach, regurgitation is the snake's instinctive reaction.

A rule of thumb for corns regarding meal size is not to feed any food item that is 1.5 times larger than the girth of the snake. I recommend not feeding more than one item at a time unless the food items are smaller than the above rule. Not only is regurgitation a common result of overfeeding, but obesity is the primary reason for poor breeding performance in corns. It also shortens a snake's life from heart disease and digestive complications.

Rough or excessive handling can also cause the regurgitation of a recently eaten meal. It's a good idea to let your corn relax and digest for at least 48 hours before handling. Most corns can tolerate handling after this digestion period, but if your snake regurgitates after this resting time, practice post-regurgitation therapy and wait longer after feedings before handling.

If your corn shows signs of shedding, skip this week's feeding. The seven to ten day duration of a shedding event without a scheduled meal will not adversely affect your snake. It's better to avoid a potential regurgitation by not feeding during this time than to deprive your corn of nutrition for several weeks while instituting post-regurgitation therapy.

It is not uncommon for corns to regurgitate from being in close proximity to a cage mate or an animal outside their cage. In fight or flight scenarios, snakes often regurgitate a meal so they are better able to fend off a predator or flee from it faster with an empty stomach. A good reason for keeping just one corn snake per cage is the elimination of this potential stimulus. Put your corn's cage in a location in the house where it will not be able to see or smell other household pets.

Just as it is with mammals, internal parasites and diseases can cause regurgitation. This does not mean you should suspect a systemic problem if your snake regurgitates. A corn snake maintained properly is less apt to contract a disease than almost any other species of pet. I have friends that boast having corns for over 15 years without ever having a single medical problem. Still, it is wise to ask your friends which veterinarian in your area has a good reputation for treating reptiles BEFORE you have an emergency. Prompt reaction to any medical problem can sometimes mean the difference between life and death. In the **HOUSING** chapter, some of the most common toxins were discussed. Besides avoiding the use of those cleansers and air fresheners, use common sense when exposing your corn to anything outside its cage. Do not medicate your snake. Leave that to a qualified veterinarian who knows what drugs are safe for reptiles. Do not feed your corn any meal that does not smell fresh. Don't risk your snake's health for the sake of feeding an overly thawed or spoiled rodent. Water borne pathogens are the most common ailment in corns, so change the water in the cage frequently.

External Parasites

Mites and ticks subsist on the blood of animals. They consume blood through sucking mouth parts they insert into their host. Since the scales of snakes are relatively impenetrable, most ticks and mites burrow between and beneath scales to access the soft skin. Besides random populations anywhere on the snake, these parasites sometimes concentrate in the longitudinal expansion flap under the chin of the snake, and around the eyes and vent.

The skin around a corn's eyes is a common place to find ectoparasites such as mites.

Mites

One of the simplest ways of detecting mites on your snake requires a white cloth bag. Place the corn in a clean white cloth bag for one to two hours. Upon removing the snake, closely inspect the inside of the bag. The most common mite found on corns is the snake mite, *Opyionyssus natricis*. The snake mite prefers reptiles so it is seldom a parasitic threat to birds and mammals. The general appearance of these mites is not unlike that of ground pepper. The adults are gray, brown or black. Depending on age, gender and vitality, adults range in size from 1-2mm. The macroscopic legs of this tear-drop shaped arachnid are so small, they are barely visible to the naked eye. Due to their prolific nature in ideal conditions, even a modest population of mites could lay thousands of eggs daily. The eggs are deposited nearly everywhere in the cage (and on your snake) and are capable of lying dormant for many weeks. The importance of quickly exterminating mites cannot be overstated. Besides the potential for disease infection, the loss of blood your snake experiences can result in lethal dehydration and anemia. It's not uncommon for a neonate corn to be killed in a matter of days from unchecked mite infestation. Therefore, if mites have been discovered, I recommend cleaning and disinfecting the cage and accessories on a daily basis until no parasitic evidence remains.

There are several methods of eradicating mites, but persistence and diligence are paramount. Regardless of what procedure(s) you employ, the first thing to do is vigorously wipe the snake repeatedly with a damp cloth under running water in a head to tail direction. The water should feel slightly cool. Dry the snake with paper towels and dispose of them immediately. Place your corn in a clean container while you disinfect the cage and all cage accessories. Hot, soapy water will kill most of the mites, but a dilute bleach solution (as little as one teaspoon per gallon of cool water) can have a residual killing effect. Hot water kills mites, but speeds the evaporation of bleach so the cool, dilute bleach solution should be applied after cleaning. Allow the cage and all accessories to dry for several hours before reintroducing your snake. Keep cage accessories to a minimum until you eliminate the parasites. The eggs of mites can lie dormant in the creases, cracks, and porous surfaces of the snake's cage and cage decorations.

Caution: Do not apply bleach solution onto your snake.

Your corn's natural instinct to rid itself of ectoparasites is to soak in water. This will kill many of them, but some will survive this process by migrating to the head. Place your snake in a container of cage-temperature water. This container must have a closure, but air holes are needed to ensure adequate ventilation. The water should be slightly deeper than the height of your snake. The idea is to allow the complete emersion of the snake except for the head. A few drops of liquid dish detergent added to the water will facilitate the drowning of the mites and will not be harmful to your snake. Allow your pet to soak in this solution for about one hour per day for four days. Some of the mites that were not drowned may not be attached to the snake by their mouth parts, so immediate rinsing under running water will wash them away before they can reattach themselves.

Since there are a myriad of microscopic pores on all surfaces of the cage and accessories, cleaning never kills all the parasites and their eggs. Therefore, the use of pesticides is the next logical strategy. There are many different products available in the reptile industry. Consult friends or the Online chat forums for suggestions about which ones are safe and most effective. Follow manufacturer's recommendations for dosage and application. Many such products are not recommended for direct application to your snake. Avoid exposing your snake to any insecticidal product during a shedding process. This is when snakes are most susceptible to toxins and such products used to kill mites could be absorbed by your corn in dangerous concentrations. The proliferation of these parasites is extraordinary so it's obvious that you must eliminate them everywhere. If they were in the cage and on your snake, it's likely they are elsewhere, so practice strict hygiene throughout the room. With diligence, they can be eradicated in a matter of days.

Note: Shed skins should be removed immediately during such parasitic outbreaks as they can harbor many mites and their eggs.

Ticks

These external pests are considerably larger than mites. Some resemble dark colored, somewhat circular disks with legs much more obvious than those of mites. When fully engorged with blood, some are bulbous and balloon shaped. Obviously since they hatch from microscopically sized eggs, they can be any size from that of a speck of dust to almost ½" (12 mm).

The same procedures for eliminating mites on your snakes apply to ticks. The main difference is that ticks are not so easily washed off. In fact, it can be difficult to remove them without leaving the tick's mouth parts embedded in the skin of your snake. Left in the skin, these can cause infection, so if you remove them manually, do so very slowly and use a magnifying glass to ensure you did not dismember the tick. If the infestation is great, I recommend not removing more than 10 ticks per day. More than that can result in open sores in quantities sufficient to invite infection. Many ticks can be persuaded to release their attachment to your corn by dripping rubbing alcohol onto the tick's body. One drop is recommended since the penetration into your corn by the tick allows the alcohol to enter the snake's bloodstream. This can potentially elicit a violent reaction from your corn as the alcohol makes contact with the point of penetration, so be prepared for a lurch from the snake or even a bite of protest.

Phorid Flies

Another potential danger to corns is the Phorid fly. While disease vector is their main relationship with corns, they can be parasitic in extreme cases. This is usually only witnessed in hatching situations where dead eggs have attracted these flies. Ordinarily these flies feed on carrion, but in some cases, very young and/or weak hatchling corns can fall prey to overwhelming quantities of Phorid fly maggots. Uneaten mice in your corn's cage are irresistible to these pests. Regurgitated mice are equally enticing, but these flying vermin are even lured to feces in the cage. If your snake is infected with disease or internal parasites, the flies will transfer such problems from cage to cage as they search for mates or their next meals. The epidemic potential within your collection is akin to that of a virus. Phorid flies perpetuate so quickly and in such great numbers that a problem only one of your snakes possessed could soon become common in your collection. Even though these flies are indigenous to almost all regions of the American Continent, they rarely present a threat to the casual snake keeper. The best way to avoid dealing with these pests is to keep your cages clean. Remove uneaten rodents as quickly as possible and do not let feces accumulate in cages.

Dysecdydis (*incomplete shedding*)

Causes and treatments are outlined in the **SHEDDING** chapter.

Respiratory Infections

The most common respiratory infections in snakes are referred to as URI (*upper respiratory infections*). Lower respiratory infections are rare. Most are the result of bacterial infections. These can be caused by improper cage conditions such as inferior temperature and excessive humidity from inadequate ventilation. It can also be contracted from other infected animals or the cross handling thereof. It is usually transmitted through saliva so if respiratory infections are suspected, change water and disinfect the water receptacle twice daily. Of course, do not handle other snakes without first properly disinfecting your hands and forearms. Bacteria can be transmitted by contact with your clothing also.

Common symptoms of URI include:

* Mouth gaping
* Labored breathing

Infectious stomatitis (mouth rot) can result from unchecked upper respiratory infections. Inferior cage temperature is often the cause of this condition.

* Sneezing
* Back arching
* Excessive saliva
* Nasal discharge

If your snake exhibits one or more of these symptoms, it is not automatically an indication that is has URI but you should consider contacting a qualified reptile veterinarian.

Except for precautionary measures to reduce the chances of spreading, there is little you can do if URI reaches advanced stages. When one or more of the above symptoms are exhibited, sometimes warming the cage to temperatures approaching 90° F (32° C) can help. The immune system of corns is facilitated by increased temperatures, but allowing the cage temperature to exceed 90° F (32° C) is dangerous to your snake and only recommended if you are able to monitor temperatures constantly. Reduce the size of the water bowl and keep the cage as dry as possible. Remove moist substrate quickly. The prudent advice if URI is indicated is to have a veterinarian culture a swabbing of the saliva to determine which antibiotic will be most effective in correcting this condition.

Injuries

Captive corns are not exposed to all the dangers their wild counterparts encounter, but from time to time, injuries can occur in the cage and around the house. It's not uncommon for cage furnishings and accessories to have sharp edges that can cause cuts. Ensure that cage closures are secure. Snakes can literally be skinned alive by crawling through spaces that are too small to fully accommodate them.

Superficial cuts and abrasions to the skin should be treated much the same way you would treat minor wounds on yourself. Clean the wound with mild soap and water or a Betadine® solution. Dab it dry with a clean paper towel or tissue. Apply a light covering of a topical antibiotic salve. Most topical antibacterial ointments manufactured for humans are safe for use on reptiles. Do not use those that contain anesthetics. Corns can receive toxic levels of such pain medications when applied directly to open wounds. Wipe the site clean and repeat this treatment twice daily for one week since cage debris can collect on the ointment. In some cases, the injury may require your vet to close the wound with sutures. The wound will scar over and heal in two to three sheds, depending on the severity. The wound site will undoubtedly cause irregular shedding so your assistance in removing stubborn sloughed skin around the injury site may be necessary.

Note: Clean your hands thoroughly or wear latex gloves when treating any open sores on your pets.

Rodent bites usually puncture muscle so the risk of infection is greater. Clean the wound as you would a superficial cut, but avoid the application of petroleum based antibiotic ointments. Such medications entering the bloodstream can be slightly toxic to snakes. Monitor the wound site regularly and if discoloration or swelling occurs, consult your veterinarian.

Any injuries to the eyes or mouth of your corn present an increased risk of infection and should be treated accordingly.

Dystocia (*difficulties in egg laying*)

Sometimes during oviposition (*egg laying*), one or more of the eggs become lodged and cannot be laid. This can be caused by many different problems, but the resulting inability to lay the egg(s) can have deadly results.

Only allow healthy corns to breed. Malnourished corns can experience complications that could not only result in the loss of eggs, but can cost the corn her life in the process. Avoid stress as much as possible while she is developing eggs. She should not share a cage with any other snakes until after she has laid her eggs.

Often a female corn that is too small to lay her first clutch of eggs will fall victim to dystocia. In cases of immaturity and because of the sedentary nature of all captive corns, I recommend exercising the female for several weeks prior to egg laying. In the wild, even gravid (*egg laden*) corns will continue to travel away from their hides in search of water, food and change of temperature. In the process, they slither over rocks and branches which facilitates the toning of muscles. By conditioning the muscles around the oviduct, the female is better equipped for the demanding task of oviposition. To emulate this palpating exercise, allow your corn to crawl across your open hand and onto your other hand, over and over again. Another way is to follow your snake around the house as it maneuvers over obstacles. Five to ten minute sessions, two to three times per day will decrease the chance of dystocia in captive corns.

PHOTO GALLERY

Okeetee.

Reverse Okeetee.

Snow.

Coral Snow.

Banded Amelanistic.

Banded Abbott's Okeetee.

Striped Butter.

Striped.

Vanishing Stripe.

Caramel Motley.

Amelanistic Bloodred.

Pied-sided Bloodred.

Ghost Bloodred

Anerythristic Motley.

Pewter.

Lavender.

BIBLIOGRAPHY

Conant, Roger (1975) 2nd Ed. A Field Guide to Reptiles and Amphibians of Eastern and Central North America. Houghton Mifflin Company. Boston, Massachusetts.

Burbrink, F.T. (2002). Phylogeographic analysis of the corn snake (*Elaphe guttata*) complex as inferred from maximum likelihood and Bayesian analyses. Molecular Phylogenetics and Evolution, 25: 465-476.

Love, Kathy and Bill (2005) Ed. Corn Snakes The Comprehensive Owner's Guide. Advanced Vivarium Systems. Irvine, California.

Mader, Douglas R., M.S., DVM (1996). Reptile Medicine and Surgery. W.B. Saunders Company. Philadelphia, Pennsylvania.

Pritzel, Charles (2005). Cornsnake Morph Guide. Privately published. Mount. Prospect, Illinois. http://www.cornguide.com

Utiger, U., N. Helfenberger, B. Schatti, C. Schmidt, M. Ruf, and V. Ziswiler. (2002). Molecular Systematics and phylogeny of Old and New World ratsnakes, *Elaphe* Auct., and related Genera (Reptilia, Squamata, Colubridae). Russian J. Herp. 9, 105-124.

SUGGESTED RESOURCES

Serpwidget's Genetic Information and Tutorial
http://www.serpwidgets.com/genetics.html

Kingsnake.com, Corn Snake Forum
http://market.kingsnake.com/index.php?cat=60

Cornsnakes.com, Corn Snake Forums
http://www.cornsnakes.com/forums

German Corn Snake Almanach
by Daniel Bohle and Michael Glaß
http://www.kornnatterlexikon.de/en

Mick's Corn Snake Progeny Predictor
http://www.mywebpages.comcast.net/spencer62/cornprog.html.

There's Just Something About Corns
http://cccorns.com/Newsletter/newsletter.htm